The Gentle People:
An Inside View of Amish Life

Third Edition

by
Joe Wittmer, Ph.D.
With Contributions From
Amish Children and Adults

A Note From the Publisher

The **Black Buggy, LLC** is extremely pleased to publish the Third Edition of Dr. Joe Wittmer's book, *The Gentle People: An Inside View of Amish Life.* Since he was born here in our local community of Washington, Indiana, I know "Joe" and his immediate family well. As a person who grew up in an Old Order Amish home, I believe strongly that Joe has written an accurate portrayal of the Amish's slow-paced, stress free way of life. If you enjoy reading Joe's book, come visit us at the Black Buggy Restaurant and then take a tour of our local Amish community. I believe that such an experience will give you an even greater appreciation for the Old Order Amish and their unique values and moral code. In addition, it will also give you a better understanding of why Joe writes with so much feeling and appreciation for his Amish heritage. If you can't visit us in person, or have questions for us, check us out at **blackbuggy.com.**

Laverne Graber, Owner
Black Buggy LLC

Dedication

This book is dedicated to the memory of my Amish parents and to our grandchildren; Raechel Thompson, Haley Thompson, Colby Marshall Wittmer and Torria Sue Wittmer—may they grow to appreciate their Amish heritage.

Copyright ©2007 Joe Wittmer

Library of Congress Catalog Card No. 2004112682
ISBN 0-9715404-1-1

Publisher—

Black Buggy Restaurant & General Store
P.O. Box 667, Washington, IN 47501
Toll Free 1-877-712-8449
www.BlackBuggy.com

Graphic design—Earl Sorenson
Cover Photo— © Scott Rothstein I Agency: Dreamstime.com
(Amish Boy On Scooter)

References and Acknowledgments

A very special thanks to Chris Cleary for his constructive assistance and to the publishers of: *Young Companion, Family Life,* and *Blackboard Bulletin* (Pathway Publishers, Aylmer, Ontario N5H 2R3).

Every effort has been made to give proper acknowledgment to all those who have contributed to this book. Any omissions or errors are regretted and, upon notification, will be corrected in subsequent editions.

Table of Contents

The Author—Age 10

This photo of the author was found some time ago in the effects of a late aunt. I well remember posing for the taboo camera at about the age of ten. The cameraman was a non-Amish "driver" who had been employed to "carry" my aunt and her family from a distant Amish settlement to my sister's wedding. This is the only available photograph of me from that time in my life.

The Author

Dr. Joe Wittmer is Distinguished Professor Emeritus of Counseling at the University of Florida in Gainesville. He was born and raised Old Order Amish and remained a participant for the first 16 years of his life. His former Amish home is located in the vicinity of Washington, Indiana; home to a large group of horse and buggy, Old Order Amish people. Dr. Wittmer has written extensively regarding the Amish and is the former Vice-Chair of the National Committee for Amish Religious Freedom. He has also authored or co-authored 15 books in the area of teaching and counseling.

The Illustrator

Mrs. Sue Wittmer, M.A., Gainesville, Florida.

More About the Author/Editor: Growing Up Amish

I am often asked what it is like to be an Amishman. Most Americans know them only by newspaper reports as a simple, virtuous people, who live on farms and use no electricity, automobiles, trucks, tractors, radios, television or other such "necessities" of modern life. Their broad-brimmed black hats, black buggies and past tussles with educational authorities all have further stereotyped the Amish as anachronisms in this space age. Their values, we are told, are of the past. Better than most people, I know what the Amish really are like, for I was born and reared in the Old Order Amish faith.

Religion on our Indiana farm was a seven-day-a-week affair. The way we dressed, the way we farmed, the way we talked—our whole lifestyle—was a daily reminder of our religion, as it is for all of America's Amish.

The fourth of six children, I learned the Amish way by a gradual process of kindly indoctrination. At five I was given a corner of the garden to plant and care for as my own and a small pig and calf to raise. Amishmen are either farmers or are in related occupations such as blacksmithing and buggy-making. My father had no doubt that I would someday be a God-fearing farmer like himself, and my stepmother often added in her German dialect, "and a nice black beard like your father's you will have yet."

Because Amish parochial schools were not yet in existence, I entered the strange world of public school at eight. My parents deliberately planned this late entry into school so that I would be sixteen, the minimum age for quitting, in the eighth grade. High school, to the Amish, is a "contaminating" influence that challenges the Biblical admonition to be a "peculiar people." No Old Order Amish children are permitted more than eight years of formal education. The Amish also resist education below the eighth grade if it originates in modern consolidated schools. America was at war with Germany when I entered the first grade. Without radios and newspapers or relatives fighting (all Amish are conscientious objectors), I had little opportunity at home to keep up with the progress of the war. School was another matter.

Boys played war games and talked constantly about the war and the branch of service they someday would join. Often I was asked where I would serve. I knew that as a conscientious objector I would never go to war.

I often wished that I could help the non-Amish children gather sacks of milkweed pods, used to make life preservers for American flyers. However, I was taught that to engage in activities that would further the war effort was sinful. Because I did not participate, I was often the object of derision.

The ordeal of Amish students reached its cruel peak during the daily pledge to the flag, which for religious reasons, our parents taught us not to salute or pledge allegiance to. The jibes of students and the disappointed looks of the teacher as we remained seated cut me deeply. How could I explain that the Amish believe in praying for all governments, which, they hold, are ordained by God? How could I explain that hate is not in the Amish vocabulary? Explain it, moreover, in a German accent, for German was the first language of all Amish youth because the church required it to be spoken at home.

In retrospect, I can understand all too well the feelings of the non-Amish students. I can understand also why the Amish have established their own schools. What was at stake was not only the feelings of Amish youth, but a way of life.

Few non-Amish understand the pressures on a nonconformist in the public school system. Many activities are strictly off limits to the Amish youth; not only dancing and other "worldly entertainments," but also class pictures and educational movies. When such activities were scheduled, we Amish children were herded into another room to the chiding and laughter of our classmates.

The pressure was always on us to conform to the majority way of life. My non-Amish schoolmates were taught that, in America, good guys wear white hats, not broad-brimmed black ones. Teachers made it plain that everyone should yearn for a college education—forbidden by our religion. They pressed non-Amish values on us and sought to alter our perception of reality. Here is the American melting pot syndrome in action. The American way of life—both for the here and the hereafter— is the greatest in the world. All else is inferior and only the fool does not seek assimilation.

My most vivid memories of boyhood days concern hostility and harassment endured by my parents and others in the Amish community. Often "outsiders" attacked us and verbally assaulted us when we rode in our buggies. They threw firecrackers, eggs, tomatoes, even rocks. Soldiers home on leave burned our wheat shocks, overturned our outdoor toilets, broke windows and stole buggies. A favorite tactic was to sit in a car trunk and hold onto a buggy while the car sped down the road. The buggy was turned loose to smash into bits against a road bank. After witnessing many such acts of vandalism, I became terrified of non-Amishmen. My father and the other elders of the community refused to summon law officials to their defense, however. They turned the other cheek and prayed for them.

But if there was turmoil and conflict without the Amish community, peace was the watchword within its borders. We worked hard and we played hard, though without the competition of the outside world. Thrashing days, barn raisings and public auctions were a more than adequate substitute for radios, comic books and organized sports.

Amish families are close-knit. We worked as a unit for ourselves and for the Amish community. We played together. We ate together—no meal was started until all members were present, and dinner was never interrupted by Walter Cronkite. For security and love you cannot beat the Amish way of life.

Then why did I, at sixteen, make the decision to continue in school—the first step away from my Amish origins? The answer is not simple. It includes (1) a passion for knowledge and (2) a growing resentment toward my Amish heritage, sparked by the years of derision and scorn in public schools. Somewhere on my way to a Ph.D. I fulfilled the one and outgrew the other, leaving still some unanswered questions for the psychiatrists to wrestle with.

Perhaps my Amish kinsmen themselves have the best explanation: That strange world outside the Amish community claimed me. And, indeed, the campus on which I teach is a far cry from my father's farm. And "a nice black beard like your father's" I do not have. But there is no animosity, no shame, among the Amish that I have left. And though I live within mainstream society, I am also the former vice-chairman of the *National Committee for Amish Religious Freedom,* the organization which defended the Amish right not to attend high school all the way to the U.S. Supreme Court and won a unanimous decision.

Preface

The third edition of this book, like the first two editions, was written with deepest respect and affection for my Amish heritage. My major reason for writing the book was an attempt to reveal to the non-Amish "world" the genuine virtues and values that best depict the Old Order Amish as they exist in the new millennium. The estimated 175,000 Old Order, horse and buggy driving, no church house, Amish Americans have been largely overlooked by historians and social scientists. Authors who have written about the Amish generally view them as people of great integrity and good-will, but have often exploited their uniqueness and picturesqueness. This book is concerned with their positive, genuine values, ways, customs and moral code as observed by those best qualified to do so—*myself as a former Old Order Amish sect member along with Amish children and adults who are current participants in the Amish faith.*

For the past few years, newspapers and magazine reporters have been quoting the Amish by first and last name; contrary to the group's long held religious beliefs. Amish leaders strongly believe that to identify a member of the church as having made particular comments about a certain topic defeats the Biblical dictate to always be a person of great humility. To the Amish, to be quoted is a sign of arrogance, a "show of pride" and not the way a Christian should behave. To their way of thinking, their names are already *"...written down in heaven..."* (Revelations 21:27) and that is the only place where they should be recorded. The Amish ministers are convinced that only bad things will result from such publicity for a member. And, after an article on Amish small businesses appeared in the March 2000 issue of *Forbes* magazine which quoted and identified several Amish church members, most of the Amish Bishops in the US ordered their parishioners to stop speaking to reporters. And further, church members were asked to no longer provide the names of any Amish people to reporters, book authors, etc. In addition, an Amish Bishop whom I trust and respect wrote me specifically to request that, if I ever revised this book, to please not use the names of any Amish contributors. I have honored his request in this third edition.

I've retained the basic changes in this third edition that were made in the second edition. I believed these changes would assist the reader to a better, overall, understanding of the Old Order Amish and many readers have confirmed my belief. For example, like the second edition, I begin this edition with an expanded "Prologue" concerning some typical questions and answers regarding the basic, underlying rules for living and Biblical principles that the Amish follow to justify their way of life. It is my opinion that the readers of this book will have a much better understanding and appreciation for the Old Order, horse and buggy Amish if they first understand some of the strong, unwavering Biblical justifications for the way they choose to live their lives. In the Prologue I give the reasons the God fearing, *Bible* reading Amish live their lives in the manner in which they have chosen to live for the past several hundred years and as they continue to live in the new millennium.

I have also retained the section regarding the roles for Amish men and women, as written by an Amish minister, found in the second edition. Another section retained in the third edition is a complete analysis of the contents of the weekly, national Amish newspaper, the *Budget*. Most Amish do not subscribe to "worldly" daily newspapers or publications. Thus, the *Budget* is their main avenue of communication. Some 400 "Scribes," one or two from each Amish community, write the news of their particular community to the *Budget* offices in Sugarcreek, Ohio on a weekly basis where it is published and sent out to Amish subscribers. It is my belief that an analysis of the contents of the *Budget* gives an accurate portrayal of what day to day life is like among the Amish as they struggle to maintain their closed society within the dominate, fast-paced, secular society of the new millennium.

In addition, the same Amish teacher who gave me permission to reprint Amish school children's essays in the first and second editions, again sent me several recently written children's essays for inclusion in this edition. This third edition also includes several essays and small, original pieces written specifically for inclusion in this book (at my request) by Old Order Amish individuals.

The term "Amish," in this book, refers to those horse-and-buggy driving, no church-house, German-speaking sect often referred to as the "plain people." No attempt has been made to write about the Mennonites, the Old Order Mennonites, the New Amish, the Nebraska Amish, the Burkholders, the Beachy Black Car Amish and/or any other Amish off-shoot group. Most of my knowledge is derived from growing up Old Order Amish in Daviess County Indiana. And, it should be acknowledged that the Old Order Amish church rules for living vary somewhat from Old Order Amish community to community. Thus, certain customs described herein may not necessarily apply to all Amish communities.

Although the author is no longer Amish, all other contributors to the book are current participants in the Old Order Amish faith. The small essays appearing in **bold** print were written by Amish men, women and children. The reader should bear in mind that the Amish contributors first language was German and none has attained any formal education beyond the eighth grade as dictated by their religion. Yet, I believe that the reader will agree that the letters, articles and short essays by the Amish as reprinted herein are well-written, considering that English is a second language for each contributor!

Because the Amish oppose photos of any kind, I have chosen to have illustrations only in this book. My appreciation is extended to my wife, Sue Wittmer, for drawing these sketches.

To the numerous people who cooperated in the writing of this book, I owe sincere thanks. I am especially thankful to the above mentioned Amish parochial school teacher. Also, I am thankful to the editors of *Family Life, Blackboard Bulletin and Young Companion* for permitting the reprinting of the letters, editorials and short essays written by Older Order Amish people that appeared in the first edition and again in this expanded version.

Joe Wittmer, Ph.D.
Gainesville, Florida

Section I

28 Questions About Amish Life and the Bible

This section includes some questions and answers regarding the Amish including the major Biblical principles underlying their religion. I urge the reader to read this section carefully prior to beginning a general reading of this book.

It is my opinion that a much better understanding and appreciation for the Old Order, horse and buggy Amish principles, standards, values, moral code and rules for living will result if one first understands the major principles and Biblical dictates underlying the Amish religion. This basic knowledge of the Old Order Amish faith will give you a thorough understanding behind the reasons why they live their lives in the manner they do today and have chosen to live for the past two and one half centuries since coming to America.

I often make presentations to various service clubs, Sunday school classes, schools, etc. and am often asked specific questions regarding the Amish and their way of life. Some of these "typical" questions, along with my answers, are given below *(each question and answer is dealt with in greater detail throughout this book):*

1. Are the Old Order Amish Changing?

Although some changes have occurred in the Amish culture since its founding in the 1690's, in general, their values and rules for living have remained intact since that time. That is, the *Bibles* the Amish read, Martin Luther's German translation, *Die Bibel*, and the King James Version, have not changed and neither have the Old

Order Amish, at least to any substantial degree. The creed of faith they follow today can be found in an historical document known as the *Dordrecht Confession of Faith* first signed in the Netherlands in 1632. This creed was formerly adopted by the Amish forefathers in Alsace in 1660, in Pennsylvania in 1725 and is strictly adhered to today.

The Old Order Amish are determined to preserve their chosen way of life, and, as noted, have not changed substantially since the religious sect came to America in the mid 1700's. To better illustrate this fact, I found a quote from an article, *Historical Sketch of Early Amish Settlers*, written in **1920** by L. A. Miller, an early Amish historian:

> *The Amish are people of distinctive characteristics, among them being their plainness of dress, the use of hooks and eyes instead of buttons, and plain colors in dress materials in preference to the printed varieties; their confession of faith: the inter-marriage only of members of the same faith; non-resistance of violence; the use of the ban, or excommunication; forbid the taking of oaths. They reject infant baptism, accept no public offices except those connected with the management of their schools; and their ministry (bishops or elders, ministers, and deacons) is chosen by lot from the congregation. Concerning their marriages, the names of the couples are always published in advance, usually a week or two weeks before the ceremony, and both bride and groom are required to be members of the church.*

If I were to write a brief description of the Old Order Amish today, some eighty-five (85) years since the above was written, I would not change a word! As a late Amish uncle of mine used to say: **"We don't want change. We have stood still for centuries and we will accept nothing new."**

Since their *Bibles* will never change neither will the Amish. There is no other way to say it, the Old Order Amish have an unequivocal belief in the *Bible* as it has been interpreted for them by their forefathers and current Bishops. They never question or waiver where their Biblical principles are concerned. If the Amish believed in bumper stickers for the backs of their buggies, they would agree wholeheartedly with the one I saw recently on the bumper of a car which read; *"If it's In The Bible, God said it, I Believe it and That's That!"*

2. Are all Amish Groups the Same?

No, there are several different "Amish" groups and various "off-shoot" groups in existence today in some 30 US States, Canada and various South American countries. Among the "off-shoot" groups are the Beachy (Black Car) Amish, the Burkholder Amish, the New Amish, the Conservative Amish, the Amish Mennonites and several more. *However, as stated in the preface, this book is about the Old Order, horse and buggy Amish.* In general, I refer to the Old Order Amish as simply "Amish" throughout this book.

Each specific Old Order Amish community (known among the Amish as a "settlement") is divided into geographical church districts of some 35-45 families each. Since large families are common (8 to 9 children each on average), each church district usually consists of between 250 to 350 men, women and children. There are no church houses or buildings of any kind that will have been built specifically for the purposes of worshiping God. The Old Order Amish meet for church and other religious ceremonies in members' homes (see below).

The Old Order Amish "rules for living," a specific church's *Ordnung* (German for "church orders or rules for living" and pronounced "ott-nung"), vary somewhat from church district to district and from Amish community to Amish community. Although they are similar in their beliefs and "rules for living," an adjacent church district (within the same Amish community, and maybe just across the road) may, for example, permit thin rubber treads on their buggy wheels while the neighboring church, just one mile over, may permit only steel bands on their buggy wheels. Another example of these differences often centers on top buggies. For example, while one church district may ban tops on their buggies altogether, another may permit them for everyone, while a third, next-door, neighboring church district may allow top buggies for all members except the unmarried men, etc. However, all Old Order Amish groups follow the same, basic Biblical principles and reveal a strong, unwavering, and tenacious belief in the *Bible*.

3. Why do the Amish Reject the Modern World so Vehemently?

Rejection of the *"world,"* as Biblically defined, is basic to the Amish religion. And, to truly understand and appreciate the Old Order Amish, one must first understand that everything they do, seven days a week, is based on the *Bible*. In my opinion, the Biblical tenet they follow most diligently, and the one that most profoundly and appropriately depicts the overall belief and philosophy of the Old Order Amish religion, is the verse that instructs them to be *"different"* from the *"world"* and to be a *"peculiar"* people (Titus 2:14). My Old Order Amish father, now deceased, used to love to say that the *"world"* began at the last Amish farm house on the edge of our settlement and that all Amish should remain *"different and apart"* from it.

An Amish sect member who wishes to remain in good standing with the church has no alternative but to be *"different from the world"* in *all* aspects of life. That is, the above *Bible* verse dictates that, as an Amish person, you must be different from the *"world"* in the way you dress, the language you speak (a German dialect some refer to as Pennsylvania Dutch), personal grooming, etc.

Amish sect members do not dress, speak or behave like members of the *"world."* They reject the *"world"* and work hard at remaining *"apart from... and separate from the world."* And, to the Amish, if you are not Old Order Amish, a member of an Amish "off-shoot" group, or Mennonite, you are a *"worldly"* person. Being *"worldly,"* or to be perceived as such, is not something an Amish person ever wants to be guilty of as it could result in excommunication.

Of course, the Amish have no choice but to peacefully co-exist with non-Amish people in the Twenty-first Century world that man has created. But they believe strongly that they are to; *"... live in the world but not of it."* (I Peter 2:11). In addition, they feel that the *Bible* mandates they live separate from the, *"...blind, perverted world"* (Phil. 2:15) as much as is humanly possible.

"Love not the world, neither the things that are in the world..." (I John 2:15). This *Bible* verse best sums up why the Amish choose to live the way they live: simply, without fanfare and very different from the fast-paced, stressful, ungodly *"world"* that surrounds them

4. Do the Amish Have Psychological and Physical Needs Different from Those of Non-Amish?

Old Order Amish men, women and children have the same needs for love, companionship, to have fun, to be physically safe along with other basic needs and wants similar to those of any other members of the human race. How these needs and wants are *satisfied* is the major difference between Amish and non-Amish. And, Amish and non-Amish Americans use very different methods to satisfy these basic needs.

Some non-Amish individuals have mistakenly assumed that the Amish are like them in need, or at least should want to be like them. For example, recently, after concluding a speech I had made concerning the Amish, an individual in the audience asked, *"Are you telling us that they really don't want to drive a car, that they really don't want running water and that they really don't want to own a television set or a computer? Come on, Dr. Wittmer, this is the new millennium, the 21st Century! Amish people surely must secretly want those things."* The answer is an unequivocal "no!"

The Old Order Amish *really* do not want to use our modern devices or appliances and they *really* do not want to be like us in most respects! Matter of fact, Amish relatives will often tell me how they truly feel sorry for certain non-Amish acquaintances of theirs because of the stressful lives they see them living. And, without question, the Amish attribute this stress to the "outsider's" moral code, values and their reliance on *"worldly,"* modern conveniences. They directly relate much of the stress they witness in non-Amish to the automobile, television, the computer, cell phones, etc.

5. Why Don't the Amish use Electricity?

As noted above, the Amish lifestyle is a deliberate and conscious effort to separate from the *"world,"* as defined in the *Bible*. Their goal is to maintain self-sufficiency in the midst of the turmoil that surrounds them in today's secular, tumultuous *"world."* According to my late father, Amish leaders decided, when electricity became commonplace before the middle of the 20th Century, that linking with electrical wire truly would constitute a counter-to-the-*Bible*, seamless connection, to be *"yoked"* with the *"world"* and *"non-believers."* They were convinced that this would violate the *Bible's* instruction not to be *"conformed to the world."* That decision, has of course, protected the Amish community from outside influences such as those brought into non-Amish homes via television, the internet, microwave ovens, etc. as well as from many other modern appliances and devices that rely on electricity to operate. The whir and noise of electrical appliances are conspicuously absent in all Old Order Amish homes.

There are, of course, many appliances that the *"world"* operates via electricity that can be, and are, converted to run efficiently on natural gas by some Amish church groups. So far as the Amish are concerned, the word here is "natural" in that it is not man-made. However, most Old Order Amish families with whom the writer is acquainted still use coal or wood burning heating and cooking stoves and an "icebox" instead of a refrigerator.

The Old Order Amish have become highly skilled at using natures way of producing ice during winter and then storing it in straw and specially built sheds to make home made ice cream, a real favorite among the Amish, and for use in iceboxes during the long hot summers. Winter ice cutting "frolics" have become a major social event among the Old Order Amish. I personally visited an Amish "ice shed" this past September which contained much more stored ice than would be needed to last until the coming winter freezes.

In addition, most Amish families have windmills on their farms to generate wind power to pump water, run blacksmith tools, furniture making tools, etc. Many also creatively dam up creeks to generate waterpower for use in operating specific machinery. Again, wind and water power are acceptable to the Old Order because they are a natural, Godly source of power and not connected to man made power lines which generate *"worldly"* electricity. And, whether it is generating power or for whatever purpose, the Amish will always work with God's natural way, with nature, never against it! To them, generating power in this natural manner is *"different"* from the way the *"world"* generates its power and is thus not *"conforming"* to the ways of the *"world!"*

6. How do the Amish Feel About Developing Personal Relationships with Non-Amish People?

Amish individuals are seldom completely comfortable around non-Amish people. Although they are to be peaceful, meek, different and a *"peculiar"* people as commanded by the *Bible*, they do have to peacefully co-exist with members of the *"world."* They understand that, like Jesus who was forced to mingle with non-believers, including money-changers, prostitutes as well as other sinners, they too must gain an accurate understanding of the *"worldly"* people living in their midst. They know they must learn to speak the English language of the non-Amish "English," understand their methods of doing things and learn how to trade effectively with them. But again, they must always live their lives *"separate and different from"* the ways of the *"world"* and further, not to be."*.. unequally yoked together with unbelievers... what communion hath light with darkness? Come out from among them, and be separate..."* (2 Corinthians 6:14). This latter verse is a favorite and very important dictate emphasized over and over again by the Amish ministers. It is the major underlying theme of every sermon given at any Amish religious service including weddings and funerals.

I remember questioning my Amish father about the meaning of the term *"unequally yoked."* He explained that it was similar to two horses being hitched together to pull a wagon and that one was a tame, good pulling horse while the other was not broken and therefore would not pull his weight appropriately. His point was that if a believer is yoked together with a non-believer, the non-believer will only pull the believer down to his level and/or lead him/her astray. This Biblical dictate also prohibits an Amish person from marrying outside the faith, from going into business with an "English" person, from attending high school, from having insurance of any kind, from collecting social security, pensions, etc. It implies strict separateness from the *"world"* which adds to their distinctiveness and *"peculiarity"* as a group.

Amish individuals of all ages and gender must avoid intimate connections with any "outsider," any *"worldly"* person, where and when possible. As noted above, the major tenet of the Amish religion is that *separation must exist between those who believe in God and are obedient to Him and those who are "non-believers" and not obedient.* And, one really never knows whether the "outsider" person one meets and has engaged in conversation is a believer or non-believer. And, of course, an Amish person would *never* ask a non-Amish person if he/she is a "believer." So, where possible, it is simply best not to "mingle" with *"worldly"* people. And, most certainly, one should not be a *"friend of the world"* as is clearly stated in the *Bible*.

7. Will the Amish Switch to Using a Specific Modern Convenience if the Non-Amish "World" Abandons its Use?

As noted, the scriptural dictate the Amish follow to be *"different from the world"* is highly important and central to their religion. They can logically reason that if a particular device or convenience were no longer used by the *"world,"* their using it would not violate this dictate. So, if the *"world"* were to suddenly change to a new way of doing things would the Amish then change? For example, does this mean that if the modern *"world"* begins using nuclear power and stops using electricity, will the Amish then find electricity acceptable as a source of power? The answer is a guarded "maybe." That is, if the *"world"* no longer uses electricity and the Amish decide to use it, would they still be in agreement with the Biblical dictate to *"remain different from the world?"* Some Amish elders and Bishops would probably agree and permit the switch to electricity in this case. However, another Biblical dictate strictly followed by the Old Order Amish is that; *"anything new is of the Devil."* Thus, there really is no way to know precisely what decision the Amish Bishops and elders might make regarding such an issue until it actually occurs.

8. Are There any Old Order Amish Groups that Permit the Ownership of Cars?

No member of an Old Order, horse and buggy Amish church who owns a car is permitted to remain as a member of the church. The car owner would be prayed for by the church, asked to make a public confession for purchasing the car and to sell it or face excommunication.

A man dressed as Amish and driving a car is most likely a member of the "Black Car" (they drive only black cars and either remove the chrome or paint it black) Beachy Amish group or one who belongs to a conservative Mennonite Church.

On occasion, Old Order Amish individuals can be seen riding in a car being driven by a non-Amish person. In such cases, a "hired" driver or a non-Amish acquaintance most likely owns the car. At first glance this might seem inconsistent, but the philosophy is that while owning a car would violate the principle of being *"different"* from, and not conforming to, the *"world,"* Amish people can accept rides in cars. For example, if a specific situation or event requires automobile transportation, and if it has been previously, or routinely, approved by the church, such travel is then sanctioned and permissible. Sometimes a trip must be taken to a distant Amish community for a funeral or wedding and the Bishops will have given their approval for the Amish to use a hired driver for such occasions. In addition, the Amish will pay for rides to meet various transportation needs such as travel to outside employment or for medical attention if the distance is too great, or too dangerous, for a horse and buggy. However, the Old Older Amish will not ride in a car owned by an ex-Amish church member. This is in keeping with the practice of "shunning" as is explained later in this book.

9. Are the Amish as Shy, Calm and Gentle as they Appear?

The Amish culture is void of the hustle, the stressfulness, the noise, the grandeur, the pressure and accompanying anxiety so often found among the non-Amish society. Their life is focused and purposeful and they know "where they are going" for the rest of their lives. The important things in life have long been tradition and set for Amish individuals by their parents, the church and the community. Additionally, the Amish do not worry about external standards for success and are not concerned about accumulating material things for their happiness. Growing up in this type environment results in a sense of calmness, quietness and gentleness which permeates the entire culture which is then demonstrated by Amish of every age and gender. For example, both children and adults will speak softly and shyly drop their heads in the presence of non-Amish.

Thus, Amish children and adults are truly reserved, shy, meek and introverted when in the presence of non-Amish. Some non-Amish find this perplexing and I am often asked by non-Amish individuals why an Amish person seems so shy and non-talkative when in their presence. Non-Amish should not view such demeanor as a personal affront or that the Amish person is being rude. It is simply a matter of religious belief. When Amish individuals speak softly and slowly and limit their conversation to as few words as possible when speaking to non-Amish, they are simply following Biblical dictates.

The Amish practice of limiting their conversation with non-Amish to a minimum is also one way to avoid unnecessary mingling with a *"worldly"* person, In addition, revealing extensive knowledge, for example, or talking excessively regarding a certain issue or event, would show pride in self which would be grounds for excommunication. The Amish believe they should always humble themselves, as did Jesus when he took on the form of a servant. Thus, to the Amish, such behaviors are simply "Christian" behaviors and should not be considered as unique to them. To be loud, overly talkative or boisterous would be contrary to God's teaching since such behavior reveals a lack of humility, and as mentioned above, shows pride. To the Amish, pride is a cardinal sin and is *never* a part of ones sense of achievement.

It may surprise some to learn that the Amish, when among themselves, are far from shy, meek or introverted. They have a keen sense of humor, full of curiosity, enjoy practical jokes, love having fun and are not at all a sad, dull, dour, and/or introverted group as some non-Amish writers would have us believe. But, they are not overly talkative or boisterous at any time regardless of who is present.

I recently asked an Amish friend what the Amish ministers mean when they quote the *Bible*, which they do every religious service, regarding leading a non-worldly, peaceful, and quiet life so far as possible. He informed me that the Amish value peace, tranquility and calmness and strive to live a "peaceful and quiet life."

Leading a Peaceful and Quiet Life

In the scripture we are told to be meek, to be still and to know God. We are asked by God to be our quiet selves at all times. We know that we move at a much slower pace than do the outside worldly people. I see the worldly people always moving about in a hurry but I have to wonder if they are really going somewhere important. Sometimes I wonder how they can find God in all that car traffic and cumbersome trappings of the modern day world.

We believe in peace and we don't start wars and we don't fight in them. We value tranquillity and we try not to be in a hurry. You really can't be in a hurry in a horse and buggy. We believe this is God's way and that this is what He expects from all Christians. We know that we live today more like in the days of the outsiders' great grandparents but this is what we think God wants from us. We strive to be our quiet self and sometimes it almost seems impossible to do that even in our much slower daily lives.

The *Bible* says that humility and showing our holiness is the way that Christians should always behave at all times. Also, as it says in the *Bible*, pride is a cardinal sin so Christians should never be proud of anything they do, say or possess. The *Bible* verses I know about this are in the books of Matthew and Romans which say, *"Blessed are the meek, for they shall inherit the earth,"* and *"Do not think of yourself more highly than you ought to think, but think with sober judgment."*

---

10. Why are the Amish Sometimes Referred to as "Peculiar People?"

Being a *"peculiar people"* (Titus 2:14) is a trait the Amish realize they must strive for in order to meet God's plan for them. However, this is not to imply that they are *"peculiar"* as defined in Webster's Dictionary, but more in coinciding with being *"different"* or *"peculiar"* in a religious sense. Of course, some non-Amish view them as being peculiar simply because of their dress code and for the way they live their daily lives.

The Amish understand that being *"peculiar"* is a trait for which they will sometimes suffer both humiliation and persecution at the hands of the *"worldly"* people. For example, the Amish realize that their slow moving buggies are an easy, convenient target for tomato or rock throwing mischievous, non-Amish youth to attack. They also realize that their pacifist beliefs will often bring about persecution, especially during times of war. They know that the clothing they wear appears odd to outsiders and may generate unwanted comments and picture snapping tourists. They also realize that tourists travel through the Amish community to simply "gawk" at them because they are so *"peculiar."*

In response to my question regarding this concept, an elderly Amish man wrote the following:

———●———

On Being Peculiar

We strive to be different and to be a peculiar people like God asks of us. We know God wants us to be different from the world in the way we look and live and to be "peculiar" like it says in the *Bible.* But we also know that this is the main reason the tourists come out here to take our pictures and to see us, our buggies, our farms, etc. God tells us that being different and peculiar will bring about some persecution but that is what Christians should expect. Persecution will always be a part of our lives on earth. This is written clearly in the *Bible.*

We don't blame the outsider for thinking we are peculiar because to them we are so. We don't mind them thinking this way, but would hope they would understand and not take our pictures.

———●———

11. Are the Roles for Men and Women Uniquely Different Among the Amish?

Yes, the roles for Amish men and women differ substantially. First and foremost, as noted, both men and women are to be *"different"* from the *"world"* in everything they do and say and to not *"conform to the ways of the world."* In addition, they are to be different from one another. Amish ministers often quote Deuteronomy 22:5: *"The woman shall not wear that which pertains unto a man, neither shall a man put on a woman's garment: for all that do so are an abomination unto the Lord your God."* The roles that both genders play are covered in greater detail in Section II.

12. Why are the Amish called the "Plain" People?

The Amish, the Mennonites, the Hutterites and similar Anabaptist groups are often bunched together and referred to as the "Plain People." This is due to their dress code, the way they groom their hair and the overall simple, plain way in which they live their lives. Non-Amish often are confused and refer to the Amish as "Quakers" because of their plainness in dress and looks. *And, in actuality, they do resemble Quakers, but 18th Century ones!*

As you will read in this book, it will become clear that both Amish men and women are "plain" in everything they do. For example, Old Order Amish men let their hair grow long, never "shingle" it (thin it on the sides) or part it the way non-Amish men do. And they must begin growing a chin beard (never a moustache since this is what *"worldly"* men often do) upon marriage (Leviticus 19:27: *"Do not round the corners of the hair on your head nor mar the edges of your beard."* And, for example, since outsider men wear belts to hold up their pants, Amish men must wear suspenders, and on and on. Amish women must never cut their hair and must always have their head covered with an organdy prayer veiling. In addition, women are admonished in I Timothy 2:8-9 to *"...adorn themselves in modest apparel, with shamefacedness and sobriety; not with braided hair, or gold, or pearls, or costly array."* Also I Peter 3:3: *"...let it not be that outward adorning of plaiting the hair and the wearing of gold or of putting on apparel."*

13. Do the Amish Attempt to Convert Others to Their Religion?

No, the Old Order Amish never proselytize and, except for ministers, are reluctant to discuss their faith, especially with non-Amish individuals. Actions and good deeds are very important and the Amish **do** believe that they are a constant "witness" to God by the way they dress, provide assistance to those in need (both Amish and non-Amish) and the way they behave in all matters. That is, although they live their lives so as *"to be pleasing to God"* seven days a week in all aspects of their everyday lives, the Old Order Amish are not crusaders for the "word of God." They are not out to "save" or "convert" the non-believer, especially a non-Amish one. They do not hold revivals of any sort, do not send missionaries anywhere, do not seek to bring new members to the church outside their own children and do not go door to door passing out religious literature. Their *Bible* tells them to be concerned about their own salvation and, *"..to take care of those of your own house..."* (I Timothy 5:8) both spiritually and physically. In addition, as opposed to other fundamentalist groups, an Amish person will never verbally state, "I am saved," since only God can know and make that judgement. But, they do view themselves as *"a congregation of the righteous."* (Titus 2:14).

Why don't the Amish send out missionaries? Doesn't the *Bible* urge all Christians to *go forth* and preach the gospel to others? Do the Amish churches not have mission programs? These are questions I am often asked by non-Amish who are quick to inform me that all Christian churches are mandated by the *Bible* to have a mission program. No doubt this is a controversial subject. However, the Amish believe that Jesus was speaking *directly to the twelve disciples* in Matthew 28:18-29 when he commissioned them to; *"..go and teach all nations, baptizing them in the name of the Father"* and not to ordinary people like themselves. They believe that they should be a "witness" to others in all they do; but do not view themselves worthy of taking on a role that was *specifically commissioned by Christ* to the twelve disciples; the divinely appointed apostles. To the Amish, to be an apostle means to be a messenger who was **personally sent** by Jesus to the ."*.. corners of the earth."* In addition, in John 15:27 and Acts 1:21, it indicates that to be; *"...called by the Lord"* as an apostle, one should *"...have seen the Lord...and to be chosen by the Lord."* And, to the Amish way of thinking, no person alive today, Amish or non-Amish, has physically seen the Lord and been personally commissioned by Him to be a missionary.

The Amish also interpret the *Bible* to say that, to be an apostle, one should not only have witnessed miracles but should have the power of "working miracles" as did Jesus and the twelve disciples. Thus, To the Amish, this implies one must have been an *eyewitness* to what one is proclaiming and/or preaching to the world and this is not possible for an ordinary person. However, the apostles were *eyewitnesses* and thus had no choice but to go forth and preach as commanded by the Lord.

In sum, the twelve disciples were very special men to the Amish. They do not name their male offspring after any of the disciples as no one is worthy of such an honor. Thus, in their interpretation of the *Bible*, the disciples were the only men commissioned by the Lord to be missionaries. Although they are concerned

about the evil *"world,"* to the Amish way of thinking, anybody can pick up the *Bible* and read it. That is, it is not their duty to keep telling the *"world"* to read the *Bible.*

14. Why do the Amish Reject Social Security, Insurance, Nursing Homes, etc?

The strong belief that they should physically and spiritually take care of their own, as described above, is also why the Amish reject all forms of insurance, pensions, nursing homes, Medicare and Social Security. I asked an Old Order bishop friend about this concept and he addressed the question as follows:

No Insurance, Pensions, Social Security or Nursing Homes

We will help others all we can if in need or hungry, whether they are Amish or not. We also urge our church members to donate blood regularly and most do. We will do all we can to help our non-Amish friends but it is not our way or plan to try to convert them to our beliefs. We do not go to help them so that they become saved. They have a *Bible* and it is up to them to read it.

We do not have a church mission and have no missionaries. We do believe that we should help our fellow man the best way we can. We know that some non-Amish churches send missionaries to places where there is hunger, etc. to preach the gospel and we have nothing against them doing that. But, we do not travel to the site where a disaster has occurred, for example a tornado, to try and convert the victims to our way of thinking. We go because God has said that we should help our fellow man in times of difficulty. This is why we go raise a brother's barn after it has been burned or otherwise destroyed. It is a way of life for us and we expect it of ourselves.

We also reject insurance, social security and pensions because God tells us to take care of our own. Our old people do not go to nursing homes as we take care of them until they die just like they took care of others before them. If you have insurance you must think that something bad is going to happen to you and that, if it does, God will not take care of you. We think this shows mistrust in God's power. We have an assistance committee that helps anyone who is in need of money to build a building that has burned down and such things as that.

In the *Bible*, in I Timothy 5:8 it says: *"If any provide not for his own, and especially for those of his own house, he has denied the faith, and is worse than an infidel."* In Gal. 6:2 we find: *"Bear one another's burdens, and so fulfill the law of Christ."* And, in Acts 4:35 we read that: *"Distribution was made to each as any had need."*

15. Can an Outsider Become Amish?

This is an extremely rare occurrence, but not impossible. However, it is extremely difficult, in the long term, for an "English" person to give up modern accoutrements for the extreme discipline of the Old Order Amish. Such a conversion would include formal instruction in Amish beliefs and language as well as baptism — not to mention highly, almost impossible and significant lifestyle changes. I know of only two individuals from the outside world who have joined the Old Order Amish church and remain members in good standing today. Several (the Amish call them "seekers") have made the attempt to join, but have failed. However, as we enter the new millennium, the Amish are adopting non-Amish infants on an ever increasing basis.

It should be acknowledged that, on occasion, a person born into the Old Order Amish faith will leave the church and join the Mennonites or some other less conservative "Plain People" church group. And, some, like myself, do leave the Amish church and culture for a more liberal lifestyle, and as the Amish say, "join the world." However, the latter is also extremely rare.

16. Are There any Black Amish?

I am often asked this question and for many years have been answering "no" with a musing smile. However, a few years ago a black child was born to white Amish parents in an Indiana settlement. You can imagine the shock and consternation among the Amish, who vehemently shun anyone guilty of infidelity, when this blessed event occurred. However, after further inquiry and before her excommunication occured, it was found that the new mother, who had been adopted as a baby into an Amish family, had black skinned ancestors. Thus, the genetic skin color had been transmitted through the white skinned mother to her child.

Several Amish are now adopting "outsider" babies, many with dark skin. Thus, it is just a matter of time until black Amish become commonplace in America. There are many black Mennonites.

17. What is Shunning?

Jacob Amman, who in the early 1690's was an elder in the Swiss Brethren church and a spokesperson for the Anabaptists, is recognized today as the founder of the Amish religion. Amman was the first Anabaptist of record to practice the shunning of erring members. This practice of social and spiritual avoidance of the "fallen member" is sometimes referred to as the "ban" (in the Amish German it is known as the *Meidung*). Every Old Amish Church practices shunning today. It is fundamental to their religion.

The fact that the Swiss Brethren (the Anabaptist church that preceded the Amish church) had stopped shunning erring members resulted in the founding of the Amish religion. Jacob Amman, the above mentioned church leader, felt that other leaders of his church "had lost their way" by not initiating this practice. Amman actually excommunicated several Swiss Brethren church ministers and ordered them shunned by other members of their own church when they refused to go along with his notion of *"Meidung."*

To the Amish charter, separation must exist between those who are obedient to God and those who reveal pride and are disobedient by not following the *Ordnung*. Therefore, a continuous tension exists between the obedient and the disobedient . The behavior of individuals has great significance in everyday Amish life and loyalty to God is judged by obedience and conformity to the church rules of discipline. Those members who break the rules must confess their sins, be forgiven and then reinstated. Those who break the rules and do not publicly confess their sins and seek forgiveness, are then "shunned" by other church members until they do confess their sins.

The Amish work at maintaining the purity and the unity of the community. Thus, in a nutshell, shunning is the process whereby disobedient members (the Amish refer to them as "fallen members") are temporarily (until they confess their sins publicly to God and to the church) expelled from the church. Disobedient members cannot be part of the *"bride"* offered to God and they are the *"old leaven"* which must be purged from the group (I Corinthians 5:7). Twice each year the church-community enacts the necessary ritual to cleanse and purify the corporate body through the observance of communion. However, one cannot commune with, or *"break the bread, drink the blood of Christ or wash the feet"* of a disobedient member.

The notion of a religious group ostracizing a fellow member via total social avoidance seems to "fly in the face" of Christian behavior. Thus, shunning is usually misunderstood by non-Amish and is often characterized as intolerable treatment of disobedient church members. However, in defense of the Amish, this is not factual and is certainly not the way the Amish view this practice. It should be understood that this is their way of bringing a "soul" back into the *"fold of Christ."* And further, this is dictated by the *Bible*, is the way it has "always been" done, and to do differently would not be "pleasing to God." As noted, the Amish believe strongly that they are to follow the "dictates of the old way" and that "anything new is of the Devil." To give up the practice of shunning at this point in Amish history would undermine their very existence.

Amish members who break the rules are given the opportunity to make a public confession and to "get right with the Lord and the Church." One who refuses to make the public confession and repent is then socially avoided (no one eats at the same table with him/her, sleeps with him/her, etc.) until the public confession and repentance occurs. Of course, members in good standing must "accept" the confession *"before man and God"* and agree, usually by standing, that it was indeed a true confession and that he/she is now back into *"the fold of God's children."*

18. Why do the Amish not Permit Photos?

Not permitting photographs of any kind is another one of the basic Biblical principles underlying the Amish faith. This may seem trivial to some non-Amish, but its importance to the Amish cannot be overstated. The Old Order Amish forbid photographs of them being taken based on the commandment that states, *"Thou shall not make unto thee any graven image, or any likeness of anything that is in heaven above, or that is in the earth beneath, or that is in the water under the earth"* (Exodus 20:4). My mother used to explain that it was difficult for an Amish person to go to heaven if a photo, *"a likeness,"* of their face was in existence upon their death.

I am often asked what the Amish thought/think of the movie *"Witness."* In actuality, they vehemently opposed the movie. And, they truly fear the *"running likeness,"* a film or video, and thus would never watch the movie. However, if you talk to Amish regarding *"Witness,"* many will know intricate details about the movie, will accurately describe the plot, etc. Most likely, some non-Amish individual such as the one whom delivers their milk to the dairy, their mailman, or salesperson has provided them this information. However, even though they have only second hand knowledge regarding the movie, they will be quick to inform anyone who asks that it is of no value and that it never should have been made.

Note: If after you read this book you decide to become a tourist in Amish country, I hope you will abide by this highly important principle and not take still pictures or videos of Amish people of any age or gender.

19. Why do the Old Order Amish Reject all Formal Schooling Beyond Grade Eight?

As noted previously, the Amish have for many years (dating back to their first days in America) rejected the notion of "too much education" for their youth. *"Worldly wisdom makes proud..."* (1 Corinthians 2) is an often referred to *Bible* verse by the Amish ministers. To them, an eighth grade education culminating at around age 14-15 is sufficient. That is, although they continue serving both formal and informal apprenticeships after that time and until they reach at least age 16 (the legal school quitting age in most states), formal, academically oriented education ends with the completion of the eighth grade. However, this does not mean that a member of the sect should be ignorant or non-educated. As a matter of fact, illiteracy is non-existent among the Amish. In response to my question regarding the Amish and education, an elderly Amish man wrote the following:

————————●◄———————

The Amish and Formal Education

It is important to be educated, but what matters most is what you are educated in. It certainly should not be in the ways of the "world" as this will lead one down the wrong path. But, like in Matthew (Matt 10:16) it tells us to be *wise as serpents and harmless as doves.* However, one should not strive to become clever and that is something you can read in Corinthians where it says; "*God traps the wise in their cleverness.*" (I Corinthians 3:19).

We believe that it is important to be well educated, especially about the *Bible.* A man never knows when he may be chosen by lot and obligated to be a minister of the church for the remainder of his life. One must be well educated in the *Bible* to be a minister. Also, we believe that we should first train our children for Heaven and then for adult life as an Amish adult. Too much education is a sidetrack from that goal.

The *Bible* states that one should (Deuteronomy 6:4-7): "*Teach the Lord's words diligently to your children*" and in Proverbs 1:8 it says: "*The fear of the Lord is the beginning of knowledge.*" The fear of the Lord is the most important knowledge one can have. But, too much "*worldly*" knowledge or wisdom ...*is foolishness with God.*"(I Corinthians 3:19). If you get too much education you become more independent and that is not good. In the *Bible* it mentions not putting a lot of trust in knowledge. If you get too educated you won't need dependency on God any more. We think that would spell trouble for our youth.

So we have our pupils go to school until the eighth grade only. After that they go into an apprenticeship with a skilled craftsman, or work on the farm and keep a journal. This ends at age 16 when formal schooling ends.

———————•———————

20. Why do the Amish Reject Infant Baptism?

The rejection of infant baptism became the most important symbol of the early Anabaptist movement, a movement the state authorities of that time considered seditious which marked the unbaptised child's parents for death. The Anabaptists argued that a child was born innocent and without sin. And, since an infant does not have knowledge and is not yet at the "age of reason," it cannot have sin and does therefore not need baptism for the removal of sin. The Amish believe that the *Bible* informs them that one must confess their belief in God and can then be baptized. Thus, infants are clearly ineligible for baptism.

In January 1527, the Anabaptists held their first baptism of adults who previously had been formally baptized as infants in the state church. It was because of this practice of rebaptizing adults that they were given the name "Anabaptists" or "again-baptizers." This practice resulted in their being declared heretics by the Catholic and Protestant churches, and, as noted, hundreds were imprisoned and/ or put to death.

Whereas both the Lutheran and Reformed branches of the Reformation maintained a close tie between the church and the state, including the practice of infant baptism, the Anabaptists believed that only adults who had confessed their faith should be baptized. For them, the state could have no part in controlling or directing the activities and teachings of the church. This led to a bloody and deadly period for the Anabaptists at that time in their history (see Section II).

Old Order Amish baptism occurs, the first and only time, at the "age of reason." It may amaze the reader to learn that this does not occur until between the ages 17 to 20 for either males or females. The Amish permit, albeit reluctantly, a "casual time" for their youth prior to their baptism. This is sometimes referred to as "running around" time, a carefree time, especially for young men, and usually occurs between ages 16 and 18 and just prior to baptism into the church. Baptized members of the church indicate that these youth are simply experimenting with the frivolous ways of the "world" and that they will "sow their wild oats" and return "to the fold." Some 85 to 95% do negotiate this "casual" time without a problem and are then baptized by the church into full membership.

To the Amish, the following two scriptures clearly state that infants and young children should not be baptized: 1 Acts 2:38: *"Repent, and be baptized every one of you,"* and 2 Acts 8:37: *"If you believe with all your heart, you may [be baptized]."* Children do not have knowledge of, nor do they understand either "repentance" or "believing" and must therefore not be baptized.

21. Why do the Amish Practice the Ritual of Foot Washing?

Twice a year, during communion services, the Old Order Amish church members get down on their knees and, with their bare hands dipping into a bucket of warm water, wash the feet of another Amish person of the same gender. I asked an Old Order Amish Bishop friend of mine to cite the reasons for this long held practice and he wrote me the following:

————————•◄————————

The Washing of Feet

We wash one another person's feet twice a year during communion services. Of course, men wash the feet of another man and the women wash another woman's feet. This is an act of love and something that Jesus did on a regular basis. Some English churches say this practice was done during the Lord's time on earth because of the type of foot wear used in those days. But, we think the washing of others' feet is made clear in the *Bible* when it says in John 13:14: *"You also ought to wash one another's feet."* We don't think it can be made much plainer than that.

————————•◄————————

22. Why do Amish Men Greet one Another With a Kiss?

When Amish men meet they greet each other and exchange the Holy Kiss. This is based on I Corinthians 16:20: *"Greet one another with an holy kiss."* This Biblical dictate is also found in Romans 16:16: *"Salute one another with an holy kiss..."* This is a routine practice among the Amish, but would not be done in the presence of a non-Amish person.

23. Why do the Amish Reject all Oaths?

According to the Amish, man owes allegiance only to God, and never to another human being. The Amish will "affirm" but will not swear to anything at any time, verbally or in writing. Writing, for example, *"I, Paul Wittmer, hereby confirm that my yes means yes"* and a handshake closes a deal. According to them, the oath is a confirmation among those who are quarreling or making promises. The Amish believe strongly that Jesus, who taught the perfection of the law, forbids all swearing. One's speech shall be *"yea or nay"* as it states in the *Bible*. Anything more is evil and not something a Christian should ever do.

24. Have the Amish Always Rejected Military Service?

The Amish have been pacifists since their founding and have never wavered on this principle. Any Amish person that becomes involved in any manner whatsoever with the armed services will be excommunicated from the church and shunned.

I also asked the Amish bishop mentioned above to expand on this question. He wrote me the following response:

———————●———————

No Military Service

As we do today, our Anabaptists forefathers rejected all forms of military service. We appreciate our government for making this a voluntary thing as it was causing us lots of hardship when we still had the Selective Service during the two world wars.

I often have to wonder how a Christian who reads the *Bible* can ever take up arms against another man, or to kill another man? This is clearly against God's will. The *Bible* makes this so clear to us when it says, in Matthew 5:44: *"Love your enemies."* We think this is also made clear to us in John 18:36: *"If my kingdom were of this world, then would my servants fight."*

———————●———————

25. Why do the Amish Reject the Courts and all Litigation?

The Amish will always *"turn the other cheek"* as dictated by the *Bible*. They do not protest publicly and will never employ an attorney for any transaction. According to their interpretation of the *Bible*, if an Amish man has a disagreement with another Amish man, the two will each choose one or two additional men to meet with them (the two disputants) concerning the disagreement. Following a discussion among the group of men, a vote will be taken and the majority rules. If in the unusual case that this does not end the disagreement, it is taken to the church as a whole (Matthew 18:15-17).

The above mentioned Amish Bishop cited the following Biblical reasons underlying this Amish standard as follows:

———●———

The Rejection of Lawyers, Courts and Litigation

We reject worldly litigation and the courts because we are asked by God to be *"Defenseless Christians"* and to *"Turn the other cheek."* The Lord tells us not to protest if they stop up our wells but to find new lands to move to and some of our people have done just that to escape religious persecution. King Solomon, the wisest man to ever live had this to say on how to resolve conflict, *"A soft answer turneth away wrath; but grievous words stir up anger."*

It has long been known that, at the conclusion of a war in which the US was involved, the Amish will be among the first to send CARE packages to the former enemy in the defeated country. After World War II, the Amish were criticized for being too quick to send such relief to Germany, their fatherland.

26. Why do the Amish not use Church Houses for Religious Services?

The Old Order Amish hold church services every other Sunday in members' homes. In my former Amish community, although not required, the in-between Sunday is set aside for visiting in the homes of relatives, friends, etc. The Amish Bishop mentioned above wrote the following concerning this question:

———●———

No Church Houses

No, we do not believe that God wants us to build any church houses or any building to be used only for worship services. The *Bible* says, *"God dwells not in temples made with hands"* (*Acts* 17:24).

We hold our church services every other Sunday in a different member's home. Some say we do it this way because that is the way our Anabaptist ancestors did it to avoid being caught by the state authorities. Some historians say that our fore fathers switched meeting places like this so that it was difficult to catch them. That may have been so in the old times, however, we see our home as the same as the church.

---

27. How did the Amish respond to the September 11, 2001 Terrorist Attack?

The unprecedented terrorist attack on the World Trade Center Towers and the Pentagon was a horrific, life-altering event for all Americans, including the Amish. Experts are still uncertain of precisely how this tragedy has affected America's children and adults. However, since the Old Order Amish do not watch TV, nor read the daily newspapers, I am convinced that it did not affect Amish children nearly as negatively as it did non-Amish children. But, there is no doubt that Amish adults have been forced to reaffirm their pacifist beliefs more than at anytime in history and have also struggled with how America should have responded to the horrific event. But, they were/are unequivocally opposed to the wars in Afghanistan and Iraq and do not believe that the "peace loving spirit of Jesus" ever sanctions the taking up of arms against their fellow man, regardless of the circumstances. They are well aware of the many wars described in the Bible. However, the Amish interpret the Old and New Testaments through the "words of the loving and peaceful Jesus" and believe that He meant what He said when he stated, "love your enemies." Several Amish have told me that, since 9/11/01, they have been confronted regarding their citizenship and allegiance like never before. The Amish love their country and teach their children to respect the flag. But, waving and/or saluting the flag, pledging allegiance, singing the national anthem, etc, is contrary to their interpretation of the Bible. The Amish are committed pacifists and these beliefs resulted in several documented conflicts for them with their non-Amish neighbors since 9/11/01. For example, many have been criticized and scorned for not flying the flag on their homes and businesses following the unparalleled tragedy. In sum, the Amish agree that America's war on terrorism is more complicated and confusing for them than any previous war in which the US has been involved. They, like all Americans, are trying to make sense out of the continuous terrorist threat to all of us and are still learning how to react to, and understand, individuals who wantonly kill and maim other people in such a particularity dreadful and horrific manner.

---

28. How did the Amish feel about the Reality Show: Amish in the City?

The 10 week long, TV reality show, Amish in the City, aired during the summer of 2004 and it was reported that some 5.9 million Americans (*Time Magazine*) viewed the first episode. However, Old Order Amish church members were not among these viewers as they do not own, nor do they watch, television. Thus, it is difficult to pinpoint exactly how they felt, as a group, about the TV show. I have spoken to many Amish regarding the show (most had a basic knowledge of it) and to a person, each was appalled and emotionally distressed that it was produced and broadcast nationally. The basis for the show was a simple concept: UPN recruited and paid 5 Amish youth of *rum springa* age, along with six non-Amish "city kids" of the same age, to participate in the show. The 11 youth were taken to Los Angeles where they lived together in the same house for several weeks where they were filmed interacting during free time and while engaged in structured activities.

As delineated elsewhere in this book, many Amish youth go through the "running around time" known as *rum springa* and most (some 85-90%) successfully negotiate this "causal time" and return to the fold. This important rite of passage begins at age 16 and prior to baptism into Amish church membership. Some Amish parents do tend to "look the other way" during *rum springa* and see this as a very important decision making time in the life of their offspring. Some Amish youth do run into difficulty with the "world" during this phase of their life. That is, some tend to experiment with, as the Amish say, some of the "frivolous" aspects of the modern world. However, the reality show producers led its viewers to believe that *rum springa* is a church sanctioned practice whereby Amish youth are encouraged to experiment with the aspects of the "world." The fact is, no Amish congregation sanctions the *rum springa* period as a time when their youth are so encouraged. Simply put, *rum springa*, in the Amish sense, is a time when their youth become adults, "put away the things of a child," and become of dating age (16). Thus, the Amish believe, as I do, that the myth surrounding *rum springa* was further perpetuated by the show and, additionally, that the non-Amish viewers were seriously misled in regards to the genuine virtues, values, ways and moral code of the Old Order Amish.

Section II

Introducing the Old Order Amish

Brief Description

"I think they are beautiful people. They are so sober, The way they think, the way they feel, the way they dress—it is all one unit. They mind their own business and live their own life and I think this is beautiful."

These are the words of Mauricio Lasansky, the artist of the famous intaglio portrait, "Amish Boy," in his description of the more than 175,000 Old Order Amish people scattered throughout 24 states and Canada. Many people confuse the Old Order Amish with the Mennonites, Amana, Hutterites, Beachy's and other type religious off-shoots of the early Anabaptist. This book is about the Old Order, no-electricity, horse-and-buggy-driving Amish. Obviously, like any other culturally distinct group, the Amish may have a negative side; however, I have chosen to focus on the positive in this book.

It is difficult to pinpoint the exact number of Old Order Amish people living in America today. However, we do know that at least 32,432 Amish children were enrolled (several schools did not report their enrollments) in Amish schools (grades one through eight) during the 2000-2001 academic year (*Blackboard Bulletin*). Amazingly, this is a 40% increase in Amish school enrollment since 1990! Some Amish children attend public schools until completion of the eighth grade. Thus, I estimate somewhere around 160,000 Old Order Amish living in the US with probably another 10 or 15 thousand more living in Canada and South America for an estimated total population of 175,000. The largest concentration of Amish, more than 40,000, dwell in a five county area surrounding Holmes County, Ohio (USA Today, April 15, 2005).

The values of peace, total nonviolence and humility are in evidence in any Amish community. They do not teach the skills of violence and technology. An Amishman realizes early in life that he is totally non-resistant and that he will never go to war. These values, lived by the Amish adults, gain the allegiance of the Amish youth; few permanently leave the sect. Further, there is no indigence, divorce or unemployment. There is very little delinquency and no record of an Old Order Amishman being arrested for a felony and none have ever appeared on a welfare roll. The Amish also value calmness and tranquility—how can you be in a hurry while driving a horse and buggy?

Our Driving Horse

Our driver is almost red. He is a nice horse and he takes us where we want to go. Some horses kick, but old Jamie doesn't. I sit in the back of the buggy and I get scared when the cars come. They get close and make dust. Once Uncle John's got hit and the driver died. I was sad. Uncle John was hurt....

Mary, third grade

The Amish are unique and picturesque; they strive to follow the Biblical dictate to be a "peculiar people." They want no part of the values and ways that exist in the modern world about them. They wish to be left alone to live their lives away from the mainstream of the secular society. The following poem, written by a sixteen-year-old Amish female depicts the tranquility of one part of the Amish way of life—that of using a horse and buggy as a mode of travel instead of a car.

A Buggy Ride

Who'd want to drive a motor car
    When he could have a horse?
There may be many others who
    Would take a car, of course.
They do not know the joy of it,
    A horse and buggy ride.
The feel of wind upon your face,
    No stuffy seat inside.
Along the road we hear birds sing.
    And watch a squirrel dash,
And just enjoy the scenery
    Instead of rushing past.
The sound of horses' trotting feet
    Is music to the ear.
No car is ever half as nice
    At any time of year.
True, winter's snows are very cold
    And rain makes me quite wet.
The wind can be uncomfortable—
    Our fingers freeze, and yet
I still would choose a buggy ride,
    In spite of cold or heat.
I shall insist that it is true,
    A buggy can't be beat.

R., Age 16

Young Companion

The Old Order Amish strive continually to remain different from the "other people," the "outsider" or the "English" as non-Amish are called. They shun the use of television, radio, telephone and most other modern technological luxuries; they travel via horse-drawn carriages. Their homes are extremely plain and lack running water, electricity, refrigerators and most other conveniences that are found in modern American homes. Their within-group conversations are in a German dialect and they wear home sewn garb reminiscent of eighteenth century Quakers. And, as a fourth grader writes, **"We don't have TV like the English do."**

No TV

I know why we don't have TV like the English do. We Amish are different like God wants. The English can have their old TV because it's not good for you. Mom and me were in Sears one day and I saw TV a bit. Mom said they use bad words and dance on TV. We didn't watch any more. I don't want TV ever in our house.

Amos, fourth grade

The first Amish came to America and settled in the William Penn colony around 1737. Twenty-one Amish arrived on the ship *Charming Nancy* on or about October 8, 1737. Three of these new arrivals were named "Miller," my mother's maiden name. However, the first "Wittmer" (Daniel) did not arrive until 1854.

History indicates that hundreds of Amish and members of other Anabaptist sects were burned at the stake or beheaded during the fifteenth and sixteenth centuries throughout Europe. The Anabaptist were especially persecuted for their rejection of infant baptism and refusal to bear arms. *The Martyrs Mirror*, a 1,582-page book found in many Amish homes, contains a careful record of hundreds of Amish martyrs (several were named

The Old Order Amish have the reputation of being excellent farmers and they do all their farming with horses or mules. Although tractors may be purchased for use as belt power, the wheels will be removed and the tractor will be mounted on a wagon and pulled from job to job by horses.

"Wittmer") and how they met their deaths. There are accounts of the severing of hands, tongues, ears and feet, plus many eyewitness accounts of crucifixions, live burials, stake-burnings and suffocations. These accounts are related over and over again to Amish children by their parents, elders and teachers. Amazingly, this past persecution has been an important element in Amish historical memories. It has helped to keep alive their present sense of distinctiveness, and has definitely contributed to their group cohesiveness.

A World War II Scare

My dad was a 10 year old little boy during World War II and he has some scary stories to tell about that time in his life. One he tells is how the military planes seemed to scare him much more than they did his brothers and sisters. He had told his older brother Levi that he would never believe that there were actually men in those planes until he one day saw one on the ground with a man driving it. He told me that he always ran for the barn or house when the planes flew over their farm. But, the most upsetting thing to my dad was to be awakened at night by the noise of the planes overhead. To try and get away from the sound that he really did not like, he would crawl under the bed trying to hide from them. Why did he do that? Because his older brother, just making fun, had told him that the planes were carrying big bombs and that they might decide to drop one on our settlement just for practice since the Amish didn't believe in war and wouldn't fight back.

Dad's parents lived less than two hundred miles from a large military airplane base so there were a lot of planes coming and going all the time, both day and night. My dad said he spent a lot of time under the bed when he was a little boy!

Moses, seventh grade

———————●———————

The Old Order Amish are an austere people who live a simple agricultural life. In Europe they were considered excellent farmers and were sought after as tenants. They brought several new methods of farming with them to the William Penn colony. Every American community to which they migrated benefitted agriculturally.

A young Amish participant learns early in life that there is both an "Amish" and an "outsider" or "English" method of obtaining need satisfaction. They learn that deviant behavior results in clashes with their respective consciences and with peers and adults. Amish youth are constantly inculcated into a sense of martyrdom and realize the very real possibility of suffering at the hands of "non-believers." Parents vividly relate stories from the martyr book regarding the terrible sufferings of their forefathers. There is a pervasive tendency among all Amish to distrust the "English."

Amish History

...Our teacher told us about the early days and how other religion people hurt and killed our forefathers. They did these awful things because they would not fight in the war and would not baptize their little babies. That's why we are still called Anabaptist people. I sometimes dream about being killed because I'm Amish and it scares me....

Elam, fourth grade

The Amish sect's refusal to accept the "melting pot" concept has made them the brunt of much hostility and harassment and it is becoming increasingly more difficult for the Amish to preserve their peace-loving values in America. Many Amish feel that their simple, pious life is threatened by the turbulent society surrounding them and hundreds have immigrated to Central and South America.

Mainstream society's emphasis on high-powered cars, computers and contraceptive devices is conspicuously absent from the horse-and-buggy Amish world. The Amish constantly live by the scriptural admonitions to "Come out from among them, and be ye separate," and "Be ye a peculiar people." The Amish live in isolated communities attempting to stay apart from the secular influences of the "outsiders' world." However, the Amish feel the pressing-in of America's emphasis on technology, violence and Twenty-first Century progress.

Amish males dress alike regardless of age—black felt hats; denim or serge trousers held up by suspenders, hooks and eyes; no shirt pockets; two-side pants pockets only and no zippers. In addition, no variance in hair style is permitted. Amish males are taught the value of hard work early in life and their lives are laid out in front of them. They will all be farmers while some will work additionally as carpenters or in closely related areas.

The New Road

The English put in a new blacktop road in our settlement. My dad thinks they should have left the old road for us or maybe some land on each side for us to drive on. Dad says horses can't run very long on blacktop and mom thinks now more tourists will come out here with cameras. I don't like the blacktop road. The cars are scary and it hurts our driver....

Samuel, fifth grade

All Amishmen are oriented toward one goal—that of eternal life. Therefore, they equate their personal pursuance of this ultimate goal with present methods of attaining it. Industry, careful stewardship, the sweat of the brow, beards on married men and German as a first language are all means to an end— eternal life. Everything they do and wear has religious significance; religion is a seven-day-a-week affair.

Uniforms of any type are taboo among the Amish and there is observable uniformity in dress. Youngsters are attired as miniature adults. There is no change in style to be concerned about and status is not attributed to the type of clothing worn. This alleviates coveting and self pride while building group cohesion. This similarity in dress also makes a deviate highly conspicuous and thus serves as a boundary-maintaining device.

Amish Clothes

...We wear plain clothes because the *Bible* says we should. Sometimes the English stare at you but they never have said anything to me about my clothes. We can be a witness for others by being plain.... I read in the last *Family Life* that just wearing plain clothes doesn't make you a Christian. I think sometimes we forget that....

Emma, seventh grade

In my former community an Amish man begins growing a chin beard the week preceding his marriage, but the upper lip and neck are kept clean shaven. This is in keeping with their non-conformity to "worldly" values and ways as an "outsider" where a moustache is often in evidence. A straight line is shaved across the back of his neck and his hair is bobbed in a "crock-like" appearance. An Amishman does not part his hair and it is not "tapered" on the sides. The men wear large, broad-brimmed black hats, suspenders, shirts without buttons or pockets, pants without hip pockets or zippers and underwear without stripes. All shirts are sewn in such a manner so as to necessitate being put on and removed by slipping them over the head. These are considered "orders" of the local church. Such "orders" may vary somewhat from one Amish community to another.

———————●———————

Something Funny

...My Dad said when he was little one time he was with my Grandpa and some English boys called them "bushhogs." Then the boys said baa-baa like a goat. I think that is funny. Dad has whiskers but nobody went baa-baa yet.

Noah, fourth grade

———————●———————

Amish women do not wear make-up of any sort, nor shave any part of their body. They wear dresses that are full-blown and not adorned with buttons, hooks and eyes, press buttons or zippers. The only means of keeping their dresses intact is with straight pins. They do not wear lacy under clothing and store-bought bras are prohibited. A female's hair is never cut, is always parted in the middle and is pulled tight without being "puffed up."

To an Amish person the "world" begins at the last Amish farmhouse. The Amish farmer has not acquired the "worldly" need for a tractor with which to farm. He may rely on a tractor for belt power, but it will be mounted on a steel-wheeled wagon and pulled from job to job by horses. He also uses horses to plow his fields and to pull his black buggy. Work is a moral and Biblical directive. Labor saving devices are mere temptations and "something new." Something new or different is "of the Devil" while tradition is sacred. Although stern it may seem from the outside looking in, the Amish are healthy and happy. They have not acquired the methods of the "world" to attain their happiness or to fulfill their needs. And, to the outsider, the Amish may appear shy and withdrawn. And, in the outsider's presence, they will most often appear so. However, they know how to have fun. Theirs is not a "frowning" culture as some have written.

As a former Amishman, it is difficult to explain the feeling of being truly different from the dominant, surrounding society. Amish youngsters are raised very carefully and certain methods are employed to protect them from the contaminating influences of the "outsider." The fact that they are different and peculiar is a continuous indoctrinating process for the young Amish. They develop a strong conscience and quickly learn that their behavior should always be for the good of the group. Once indoctrinated, it is indeed difficult to alter themselves to accept the values and ways of others without experiencing extreme psychic pain. Thus, those who do leave the sect (usually males between the ages of 16 and 20) often do so only temporarily. That is, they return, marry and become God-fearing members of the community again. Those who do leave the sect permanently must reject their family, their heritage and the values it represents. Psychologists agree this is seldom done without traumatic conflict for that individual. And, this inner conflict causes many to return to the fold.

Amish Origin

The Amish sect was born out of the religious turmoil of the Anabaptist movement in sixteenth century Europe. Their emergence was turbulent.

The Anabaptists were a unique group during that time in history. They were not directly involved in all the warfare taking place in the name of religion. However, they were in total disagreement with the Catholics, Luther and the Reformed movement. They wanted to return to a primitive, early-type of Christianity. To bring back this primitive Christianity, the Anabaptists literally accepted the *Bible* as their dictate. They made it clear to both church and state that they would stop taking oaths, would not drink and would never again pick up a sword. Further, they renounced all sorts of economic rewards and personal-type adornment. One of the major differences between the Anabaptists and the other religious groups at that time in history was their feeling that baptism was not to be administered in infancy, but should take place when the person was old enough to reason—when the individual had assumed responsibility for his or her soul. This return to primitive religion brought the wrath of the Reformers, the Catholics and several Protestant groups onto the Anabaptists. The Anabaptists were denounced as being heretics and were subjected to the death penalty. The previously mentioned book, *The Martyr's Mirror*, gives many detailed accounts of non-resistant Anabaptists and as to how they suffered persecution and annihilation.

Despite the tremendous suffering and death, the Anabaptists prevailed. They migrated often throughout Europe in their attempts to avoid persecution. There were the Mennonites in Holland and North Germany, the Hutterian Brethren in Moravia and the Swiss Brethren in Switzerland.

In the early 1600s a division occurred among the above mentioned Mennonite Anabaptists in Holland. In 1632 Mennonite ministers from several different areas in Europe got together in an attempt to heal the breach in the Mennonite Church in Holland. During this meeting these ministers drew up a Confession of Faith to which all present agreed. The historic meeting took place in Dort, Holland and the pact developed there is commonly known by the Amish and Mennonites today as the *Dortrecht Confession of Faith*. This original agreement had eighteen articles of faith and today, 380 years later, an Amish youth must agree to these eighteen articles of faith before he or she can be baptized into membership in the Amish church.

Article seventeen of these original eighteen articles of faith was a main factor which predetermined the founding of the Amish faith. In general, the seventeenth article of the *Dortrecht Confession of Faith* indicates that all erring members shall be "shunned." In German, this is known as the *Meidung*. Menno Simon, a former Catholic highly thought of by today's Old Order Amish, was the leader of the Anabaptists in Holland and his followers became known as "Mennists." The name "Mennonite" was later applied to the Swiss and Dutch Anabaptists. Simon observed the "shunning" of erring members and his writings can be found in many Amish homes today. However, the modern day Mennonites do not practice the *Meidung*. The *Meidung* indicates that an ex-communicated member should be avoided both physically and spiritually. This includes man and wife. The ruling bishop of the Swiss Brethren Anabaptist group did not enforce this seventeenth article. A split developed in the Church and the leader of the emerging group was an aggressive young man named Jacob Amman. (His followers became known as "Aman" which later changed to "Amish.") Amman, a Swiss Brethren bishop who lived in Canton of Bern, Switzerland, took it upon himself to excommunicate all those Swiss Brethren bishops and ministers not enforcing the *Meidung*. Thus, contrary to popular opinion, the Amish are offshoots of the more liberal Mennonites.

The practice of shunning played an important role in Amish history and the practice remains important today. However, the outside "world" knows little about shunning as it is seldom discussed or written about by the Amish or others.

The writer has (on several occasions) been a direct witness to a major aspect of shunning, that of not eating with the erring excommunicated member. The member(s) being shunned will either eat first, last or simultaneously in another room of the house. Everyone present realizes what is happening but no reference is made to the shunning and it is usually dealt with without fanfare and with little embarrassment to those shunning or to those being shunned. However, I have been present when uninformed "outsiders" have caused embarrassment. And it is always a solemn occasion and sadness prevails.

Non-Amish often question me regarding the practice of "shunning" and some view it as inhuman, intolerant and question why Christians would ever sanction such a process. Thus, I asked an Amish minister friend of mine to put into words how he would explain shunning to a non-Amish person and he responded by writing me the following *(he requested that I not reveal his name or the location of his specific Amish settlement)*:

———————●———————

The Practice of Shunning

After being baptized our people are committed to follow the ways of the church and the *Bible*. However, since we are human, one of us may slip and fall into error and sin and then the ban, or shunning, shall be placed on the fallen member. But, before doing that, the erring member is warned twice privately and the third time publicly, before the congregation as it says in the *Bible*. This is done before the breaking of bread for communion Sunday which we hold twice a year so that all at communion that Sunday may in one spirit and in one love, break and eat from one loaf and drink from one cup. We cannot take communion in peace with one another if a member is among us who has committed sin but has not confessed that sin.

If the erring member confesses his sin before God and the church, he then takes communion with the others who are there and we are at peace within the church and brethren of God. If not, the ban, we say the *Meidung,* is put in place and that member is shunned.

Moderation and Christian discretion should be used so that shunning and reproof may not cause the erring member to be ruined. We are to be serviceable to him or her. So, if the shunned person is in need, is hungry, or thirsty, we are in duty bound, according to the doctrine and practice of Christ and his apostles, to render him or her aid and assistance as needed. Otherwise the shunning in itself might cause his or her ruin which is contrary to the *Bible* (I Thessalonians 5:14).

Therefore, we must not treat those being shunned as enemies, but must love and help them as brethren and sisters in a Christian manner in order to bring them to a knowledge of their sins and to repentance and back into the church to take communion with all of us. Then they can again become reconciled to God and the church (II Thessalonians 3:15).

We base all this on the following Scriptures: I Corinthians 5:13: *"Put away from among yourselves that wicked person."* 2 Thessalonians 3:14: *"If anyone obey not our word by this epistle, note that one, and have no company with such a person;"*

Romans 16:17: *"...mark them which cause divisions and offences contrary to the doctrine which ye have learned and avoid them."*

Matthew 18:15-16-17: .*"..if thy brother shall trespass against thee, go and point out the fault between thee and him alone: if he shall hear thee, thou has gained a brother. But if he will not hear thee, take with thee one or two more... and if he neglects to hear them, tell it to the church, but if he neglects to hear the church..."*

> If the member who has sinned against God and the church refuses to listen to another member who is in good standing, or to the other two that were also asked to speak to him, or to the church, then the church is obligated to ."..*clean out the old yeast*," (I Corinthians 5:7).
>
> In Galatians 6:1 it also states that if the sinner does seek forgiveness, then we are to ."..*restore such a one in a spirit of gentleness.*" For us, the act of shunning and then forgiveness is made very clear in Luke 17:3: ."..*Rebuke the offender, and if there is repentance, you must forgive.*"

———————————➤ ● ◄———————————

It is clear from the above essay that the Amish are convinced beyond any doubt that the practice of shunning a "fallen" member is Biblically mandated and that the practice should not be questioned. Again, this is one of the basic fundamental principles on which the Amish religion was founded and I believe it will continue as long as the Amish religion exists. If the practice of shunning disappears, so will the Old Order Amish as we know them.

Amish Music

The songs that the Amish sing during worship service have never been placed to musical notations, and the singing is almost chant-like. The texts appear as poetry. To the uninformed outsider it must sound like mournful droning or a Gregorian chant. The songs were written during the sixteenth century by imprisoned Anabaptists, and the main theme of these old songs is of protest against wicked tyrants. The song book is known as the *Ausbund*.

The *Vorsinger* (the song leader), a male, is never selected prior to the service. Instead, the older men at the service whisper among themselves urging a certain male to begin the singing, to "lead off." However, no one wants to show pride in his singing ability and thus always declines to lead the singing on the first urging. However, with enough prodding from others, finally someone does begin (and, usually, it is the one who first declined!) In the absence of musical notations, all songs in the *Ausbund* must be learned by ear and one must be highly skilled to be the *Vorsinger*. (It also takes skill to follow his singing lead.)

It takes years to learn how to sing from the *Ausbund* and seldom do males learn the songs prior to their marriage. The songs are extremely slow, and as indicated below, some may take as long as **28 minutes** to sing. Of course, this slow pace coincides well with the slow- paced Amish culture.

The following, written by an Amish person, provides a good description of Amish church singing, and as the writer points out, to be the song leader, **"can be a major undertaking."**

Authentic Amish dolls are always fitted and dressed in traditional Amish garb and do not have any facial features. The dolls are faceless because the Old Order Amish do not believe in the use of mirrors or of the taking of photographs of men, women or children. This is in keeping with the very important Biblical dictate that states: "Thou shall not make unto thee any graven image, or any likeness of anything that is in heaven above, or that is in the earth beneath, or that is in the water under the earth" (Exodus 20:4). They feel that you have "stolen" them if you take a photograph of their face. They refer to this as a "likeness" and will sometimes object in German, "Du hasch mir gschtohle" (You have stolen me.).

Singing the Old Songs

...Singing the "slow tunes" as they are sung in Amish churches today is indeed a special assignment. The Amish have kept up and handed down these tunes from generation to generation for hundreds of years. Sometime ago there was an article in *Family Life* (December, 1985) dealing with the origin of Amish church tunes. This article pointed out that although they may be distantly related to the Gregorian chants, they belong in a class of their own.

Why do we sing in church? Is it to keep the congregation occupied while the ministers are conferring in the *"Abrote?"* Hardly! We believe it serves a necessary purpose. A farmer would not think of sowing his seed without first getting the soil in shape. Singing these old hymns can be likened to the final harrowing before planting the crop. It should help in getting our minds into a prayerful receptive mood. What could be a better way to do this than to actively join in singing these hymns?

Indications are that this type of music grew out of the early Anabaptist church music. Without beat or measure, time or rhythm, it depends upon depth and devotion, appealing to the nobler sentiments of the heart such as reverence, faith and a prayerful attitude. Appreciation for this type of music must be learned, but once its value is perceived, it will be highly esteemed.

To a person not used to singing this type of music, the first difference he will notice is that the song leader sings the first syllable of each line alone. Since there are normally 2 to 5 notes to each syllable, this can be a major undertaking, especially if he is not too well acquainted with the song.

...If you are asked to lead a song in a strange community you may be concerned because you do not know how fast they sing. This is of little importance as it will be expected that you will probably sing like you are used to at home.

Actually the one leading the song has but little effect on how long it takes to sing a song. Each community has its own pattern and there is very little variation in the length of time it takes to sing a song, regardless of who is leading.

It is always interesting to me to note how long it takes to sing *Das Loblied*. Twenty minutes is about the normal time for most Amish communities. For some of the plainer churches it takes 24 minutes and Swartzentruber groups may take up to 28 minutes.

Whatever it is in your community, it will vary very little from Sunday to Sunday...

D.W., *Family Life*

———————●———————

Jacob Amman also introduced communion services twice a year instead of the usual once a year observed by the Swiss Brethren. Further, he introduced the communion practice still held today by the Old Order Amish, that of foot washing. Amman introduced uniformity in all forms of dress. He further taught that it was sinful to trim the beard. All of these practices are observed among today's Old Order Amish. The Amman group (later known as Amish) and the Swiss Brethren Group attempted reconciliation at least twice but to no avail. The animosity between the groups was such that even as they left Switzerland together for America they refused to ride in the same boat. This gap, which began over three hundred years ago, still exists today (to a certain extent) between the Amish and the Mennonites.

Section III

The Amish Family System

Married-Pair Living

The family system is the primary unit which organizes the dominant patterns of value orientation within the Old Order Amish culture. In most all societies it is in the family where basic normative evaluations are developed. It is the older members of the family, among the Amish particularly, that funnel the cultural heritage to the younger offspring. It is their solemn duty. It is in the Amish family setting that the child first learns to respond to authority, to play roles in the cooperative structure, and to obey the norms of the sect.

Rank differences are not extreme within Amish society nor within the family structure. However, father commands the highest rank with mother being second. Sibling rank is based according to age. The older siblings often discipline the younger children, both verbally and physically.

The Amish family organization is strictly patriarchal. The Amish father raises his son in the exact manner as he was reared by his father. The father-son relationship is of a high caliber and the generation gap seldom exists. The women of the family take a back seat to the men in most endeavors and the Amish male rarely does the tasks of a female. However, women are expected to help with most male tasks. Only on special occasions such as butchering, cooking apple butter and weddings does the husband participate in household tasks. However, women and adolescent girls frequently help with the harvest of crops, especially during cornhusking, shucking wheat and so forth.

Amish married couples never show overt affection for one another in public. The Amish man refers to his wife as "her" and she makes reference to "him." However, there is mutual respect and seldom does arguing occur in front of the children.

Although there are varying degrees of cooperation between the husband and wife in fulfillment of their roles, the Amish generally adhere to the Biblical tradition in which the husband is in direct charge over both his wife and his children. Male and female roles are clearly differentiated and the woman's place is perhaps best typified by the Biblical admonition that "the head of the woman is the man."

Young Amish females know that their adult role will be that of a farmer's wife and they are taught the skills of cooking, canning and other related "housewife" chores early in life. And, in the absence of electricity and refrigeration, this is no easy task. Although they may be teachers in Amish schools for a few years, they will never hold positions in the church or elsewhere and they know that, as the Bible dictates, "The head of the woman is the man."

The following article, written by an Amish male and re-printed in part here, gives the Biblical justification for the distinct role differentiation found in the Amish family structure. And, it is my opinion that the following accurately portrays the way things are today among the Amish.

Men and Women

...In many ways the world is a man's world. Men have the advantage when it comes to the highest paying jobs, making the big decisions, of running for president. The odds are in their favor when a ranch manager is being hired. Most of the top positions in business and government are held by men.

Perhaps it is true that men have not always been as nice and as fair to women as they should have been. I'm sure they haven't. Some men have looked down upon women with scorn, as if they were an inferior kind of human. Even today in many countries, women are trodden down and misused by their husbands as if they were their slaves, or a piece of personal property.

Such an overbearing attitude is wrong. But is it any more wrong than the modern movement by women who no longer are submissive to their husbands, who want to get into roles for which God never intended them? Which extreme is more wrong? I don't think there is any difference. Neither is right.

It is not surprising that non-Christian women go on a campaign to assert what they think are their rights as humans. Without the teaching of the *Bible*, they have no guide to know what is God's intended order between the sexes. Their reasoning is that a person is a person, therefore why make a difference in any way?

But those of us who read the *Bible* should make our decisions by the Word of God, and not by human reasoning. Yet it is a sad fact that churches are strongly influenced by what goes on outside. Sometimes the influence of the world seems to be stronger than the influence of the *Bible*.

...Peter, in his first epistle, says that wives should be subject to their husbands, even if their husbands are unbelievers. What better way to win a husband to the faith than by humbly staying in her place? Matthew Henry comments on the third chapter of 1 Peter, "A Cheerful subjection, and a loving reverential respect, are duties which Christian women owe their husbands whether they be good or bad.... The subjection of wives to their husbands is a duty which has been practiced universally by holy women in all ages."

...These verses leave no room for misunderstanding. Man is to be the head of the woman. Since this is the case, it would not seem proper to have women in positions of authority where they would rule over men. This the Apostle teaches, "Let the women learn in silence with all subjection. But I suffer not a woman to teach, nor to usurp authority over the man, but to be in silence" (I Tim. 2:11-12). To the Corinthians Paul wrote much the same thing, "Let your women keep silence in the churches; for it is not permitted unto them to speak; but they are commanded to be under obedience, as also saith the law. And if they will learn anything, let them ask their husbands at home: for it is a shame for women to speak in the church."

...So far we have chosen Scripture passages that speak to women, that command them to be submissive to their husbands and respect God's order. What about the husbands? If they are to rule the household, does this mean God has appointed them to be dictators, and their word to be law? Hardly. Instead, the verses in the *New Testament* that are directed to husbands instruct them to love their wives and to treat them with courtesy and respect.

The whole world has a distaste of the woman who henpecks her husband, the wife who is determined to "wear the pants in the family." All of us have seen examples of the disharmony that can result when husbands and wives get mixed up in their roles—when the wife is the boss, and the husband is in subjection to her.

When things get out of their proper order—when women usurp authority either in the family or in the church—it is a sad situation. And yet, is it not true that the blame often comes right back to the husband, or in the case of the church, to its leaders? In many such cases the husband has failed to fill his role as the head of the home, or the church leaders have failed to hold up a Biblical standard. When man's leadership breaks down, it is no wonder that the woman steps in.

Why has the modern mother become the head of the family? I fear it is largely because Father has failed to fill the position.

...Is a woman a lesser person because she is ordained of God to be in subjection to man? Is it a misfortune to be born a girl? I am positive the answer to these questions is a strong, "No!" Yet many rebellious women would disagree with me.

Is it such a strange thing that God should ask women to be subject to men? Not at all. No one, female or male, can escape authority. From childhood, we are subject to our parents. Paul writes to the Romans, "Let every soul be subject unto the higher powers (governments)." Concerning the ministers of the church, we are commanded, "Obey them that have the rule over you, and submit yourselves."

...Life is full of authority. Being a woman means there is one more level of subjection than being a man. That is all. It doesn't mean that a woman is thereby being degraded, cheated or despised. It is simply a fact of life, like being born a girl in the first place.

Life is just as happy and just as meaningful for one sex as the other. The secret is in fulfilling one's God-given role. For most women this means being a wife and mother—a homemaker and a help mate. Many unmarried sisters find fulfillment teaching school, helping the needy or caring for invalid relatives.

J.S., *Family Life*

Farms are usually jointly owned in order to secure legal ownership in the case of death. And property, whether farm land and equipment or household goods, are generally spoken of as "ours." However, transactions involving sale or purchase are made through the husband or have his approval. However, the husband and wife usually confer before making any large purchases.

The single woman, as well as the single man, lacks status in the family-oriented community. A bachelor cannot hold church office and a spinster can look forward to a lifetime of doing other people's housework or taking in sewing. Recently, some single Amish women have begun working in hospitals, factories and stores.

A wife may get to keep the egg money for household expenses if she takes care of the chickens, but more often the money is doled out by her husband as she needs it.

Convenience foods are not purchased by the average Amish housewife. She plants a large garden and cans hundreds of quarts of fruits and vegetables for the winter. There is no freezing of food.

The wife also has responsibility for the appearance of the lawn and area surrounding the house, including the whitewashing of fences, posts and grape arbors in the Spring.

Gardening, except for the initial spading or plowing in the Spring, is the sole responsibility of the wife. There is usually a large variety of vegetables which always includes cucumbers and red beets—standard items served at the luncheon given during the Sunday services (held in private homes).

Another area which requires a large part of the wife's time is the processing of fruits and vegetables in the summer and meats in the winter. In the absence of refrigeration, this takes unique skills and much time.

Amish women are known as good cooks and the Amish people eat well, usually with an abundance of food. Breakfast usually consists of eggs, fried cornmeal mush, liverwurst, cooked cereal and fried potatoes. No meal is without bread, butter and apple butter. The typical diet is rich in fats and carbohydrates with potatoes, gravy, fried foods and pastries.

Becoming a Housewife

...Someday, I know I will be a housewife and I look forward to it. Being a housewife will be my full-time job. Mom told me that "English" women have other jobs. Not me. I'm going to be a housewife and be a good wife for my husband....

Delilah, fourth grade

Along with preparing the meals, the Amish wife makes all the clothes of the family. Yard goods, usually denim, serge, gabardine and organdy, are purchased in a nearby town for this purpose.

Men are considered more able to perform duties in public affairs and similarly women are usually silent during the progress of religious practices and ceremonies. Women never serve as church officials, on school boards and so forth.

The bulk of the husband's duties, of course, center around the production of farm products for market. The Amish farmer is known by the crops he produces. The uniformity of dress and lifestyle of Amish families make differentiation on almost any other basis impossible. However, even these distinctions are undercut by the religious emphasis on humility and the sinfulness of pride. An Amish farmer faces excommunication if he shows undue pride in his dairy herd or other possessions.

How does the Amish wife feel about her role? The following small piece written by an Amish wife best describes, I believe, the feeling of the majority.

Helping My Husband

A father really is someone. It is a serious business to be a father for God expects great things of the man. When a man marries, he must accept the obligations and responsibilities for the physical, moral and spiritual welfare of his home. God intends for the man to set the pattern for his children.

The woman is the weaker vessel and it is her duty to be the keeper of the home. A wife who tries to help her husband in every way will receive many blessings beyond measure. She must trust her husband's judgment and stand back of him.

A father is someone who needs to be feared, not as one who rules with an iron rod. It is for our protection that we obey him and respect his judgment.

After John became my husband, his life was never quite the same. God said when a man and woman marry, they shall leave father and mother and the two shall be one flesh. Few people really realize what all this includes. The husband is the provider, the protector, the delivered of his wife's body. Every man who marries takes care of his wife as a sacred trust. The husband is to be the head of the home, even as Christ is of the church. As the church is obedient to Christ so shall the wife be to her husband.

It seems at our house things don't go as smoothly when Dad is not around. There always seems to be more tension and frustrations, but when he is here, everyone feels a sense of security and protection and everything goes better. When a storm comes up, I always feel better when my husband is at home with me and the children.

At first John worked away from home but this never seemed right. The children and I would do the chores by ourselves. I remember the evening when John said, "Wouldn't it be nice to milk more cows and make our living off the farm?"

I have often thanked the Lord for letting me marry a farmer, for there are many blessings in a farm home. A faithful wife can encourage a farmer a great deal. The investment needed to start farming can frighten a man whose wife is a spendthrift.

The father is the provider and the bread earner but

the wife and children need to help all they can in the duties and labors of a home. A father should talk financial problems over with his wife. The children ought to listen in for children can often learn a lot by just listening. A lot less problems come up in homes where the husband can talk with his wife in a loving way, and where the father enjoys the children.

God expects the man to take the lead for the woman is the weaker vessel. It is her duty to make a home out of a house, where her husband can come home to meet his love, not a grouch!

There must be love between husband and wife. Remember you were each other's choice and this was your answer to a lonely heart and to supply the comfort and joy of fellowship. When two walk together, life is much happier. If one stumbles, the other is there to hold him up. If one is discouraged, the other one should give encouragement. Two people can sleep warmer than one. Two hearts can be more cheerful and happy than either one alone. Happiness in married life is something that has to be worked for, it will not come naturally.

What can be lovelier and more beautiful than a home where husband and wife and children work together for the spiritual welfare of each other?

Anonymous—Reprinted from *Family Life*

To my knowledge, divorce is non-existent. And there are no written or unwritten provisions for securing either a divorce or a separation. Marriage is supported by kinship and religious sanction. Although Amish couples do not reveal any overt signs of affection for one another when in public, they most certainly do in private. Although the notion of procreation may be upper most in their minds, it is the opinion of the writer that Amish couples do have very satisfactory intimate relationships.

Most Amish couples have several children and they realize that when they grow old the children will care for them. It is nice to grow old Amish. The older you get, the wiser you be-come and your future does not include a nursing home. The youngest son brings his bride to his parents' farm. At this time, a second residence is usually built for the parents a short distance away—the old folks get the new homes in the Amish commu-nity. The management of the farm is then turned over to the son, and the parents retire. Relationships between the two families are cordial, and even the mother-in-law/daughter-in-law rela-tionship, which is so troublesome for other cultures with patri-archal family customs, seems to be quite amicable.

In summary, once married, an Amish woman expects no public expressions or gestures of affection from her husband. She works with him to make a good life for them and their children and to gain the respect of the community. She does not have to work to keep him. Marriage is for keeps and a roving eye is not tolerated by the community.

The Roles of Men and Women as viewed by the Church

Recently, I spoke to an Amish minister friend regarding whether his particular church district had anything in writing concerning the "orders" of the church as they specifically concerned the *roles of men and women*. With the understanding that I not reveal his name or the geographical location of his Amish community, he gave me a hand written copy of the following small piece. **"This is what we hold to in my church,"** he wrote in a cover letter.

The minister also gave me permission to reprint it here. How-ever, he indicated that he was not certain where this originated and that he did not provide his own church members with copies. It should be acknowledged that the Amish are an "oral traditioned" society and things such as a specific Amish church's *rules for living* are passed along by word of mouth and are seldom in writing. However, a specific Amish church district's rules for living *(Ordnung)* becomes well known by everyone and must be followed to the "tee" by members of that particular church district.

The Amish are recognized as expert horsemen and provide their animals with excellent care. "Drivers," those horses bred for pulling buggies, are pampered and cared for especially well. Blacktop and concrete roads dictate that "drivers" be fitted with metal shoes. Although some Amish men are more expert than others, all males are taught the skill of "horseshoeing" at a young age.

Orders for Men of the Church:

- Respect and love your wife and children. Discipline children with love and understanding not harshness.

- Be a God fearing model, especially for your boys. The *Bible* says that ...*if the fathers eat sour grapes the children's teeth are set on edge"* (Jeremiah 31:29).

* Know the *Bible* well so that you may be prepared in case the lot falls on you. As the *Bible* says in Proverbs 16:33: *"The lot is cast into the lap; but the whole disposing thereof is of the Lord,"* and in Acts 1:24-26: *"They prayed and said, You, Lord, who know the hearts of all men. Show which of these two you have chosen and they gave forth their lots."*

** All men members must be well versed in the scriptures so that as ministers we can speak freely and without notes if hit by the lot to be a preacher. This is based on following two *Bible* verses: Matthew 10: 19: *"When they deliver you up, take no thought how or what you shall speak for it shall be given you in that same hour what you shall speak."* And in I Corinthians 12:3: *"Speaking by the Spirit of God. . . ."*

- Men must not cut the hair too short or shingle it thin on the sides.

- Do not comb your hair parted in the middle or either side.

- Sunday black hats must have 3 inch brim all way round. Straw hats allowed for working. Do not wear hat back on the head.

- Do not trim the beard too much or shave too low on the chin.

- Keep the upper lip and back of neck from the middle of ears down shaven clean.

- Suspenders are the only way to be used to keep the pants up—plain black only is allowed. No fancy or adorned ones allowed. No buttons to fasten suspenders. Use clips.

- No zippers on any clothing or on anything else like clothing bags. Shoes should be plain and black. String tie only. No buckles.

- No smoking or chewing and no drinking.

- Shirts bought in the store may not be worn unless the pockets and buttons are first removed before wearing. Use hooks and eyes to close. No big collars. No bright shirts.

- Pants should be home made if possible. Store bought pants must not fit tight and must have hip pockets and zippers taken off and front flap opened up and then held shut with hooks and eyes. No buttons.

- No pretty decorating rings on the harnesses of the driving horses. No fancy dashboard and no back lights on the buggy. Tops on buggies for married men only.

- Buggies are to be plain and always black. Wheels must be steel rimmed.

- No electricity in house or dwellings. Air and hydraulic power to be used. Do not use pay phones but when emergency.

*** No farm signs allowed.

**** Do not use so much English talk, but it may be used when English folks are around. Do not permit English singing to be done at the youth singings held in your home. Do not allow children to talk English in house.

- No lightning rods on the house or the farm dwellings.

- Do not have your picture taken. Try to not let children have pictures taken by the English. This is made very clear to us in Exodus 20:4: *"Do not make for yourselves images of anything in heaven or on earth or in the water under the earth."*

- Do not tell foolish stories, gossip about others, swear or take the Lord's name in vain. As it comes from the *Bible*, Ephesians 4:29: *"Do not let any unwholesome talk come out of your mouths, but only what is helpful for building others up according to their needs, that it may benefit those who listen."*

- Do not use sleeve holders or wear wrist watches. Round, plain, simple pocket watches only.

Orders for Women of the Church:

- Do not show your authority over the man. Submit to and love your husband. As it says in the Bible: I Timothy 2:12: "I do not allow a woman to teach, nor to usurp authority over the man, but to be in silence," and in Colossians 3:18: "Wives, submit yourselves unto your own husbands, as it is fit in the Lord." And, as it says in 1 Corinthians 14:35 about the woman: "If they are to learn anything, let them ask their husbands at home."

- Do not make the organdy head covering caps so small. Keep them large enough to cover the ears. Do not make bonnets so small. Always tie caps and bonnets under the chin.

***** Do not make such broad pleats in the dresses or such broad hems. Full length aprons should be same color as dress except Sunday when organdy aprons on unmarried women are required.

- Do not comb your hair high on the head. Part in the middle and do not puff it up. Do not cut your hair. As it tells us in the *Bible*, I Corinthians 11:14-15, *."..nature itself teaches you that long hair on a man is a disgrace, but on a woman it is a thing of beauty."*

- Do not wear jewelry. Do not sew lace around the skirts. Do not wear men's clothing. Do not wear English perfumes or store bought deodorants. As it says in the *Bible*: Deuteronomy 22:5: *"Women are not to wear men's clothing."* And in Isaiah 3:18-23. *"A day is coming when the Lord will take away from the women of Jerusalem everything they are so proud of— the ornaments they wear on their ankles, on their heads, on their necks, and on their wrists. He will take their veils and their hats; the magic charms they wear on their fingers and in their noses; all their fine robes, gowns, cloaks, and purses; their revealing garments, their linen handkerchiefs, and the scarves and long veils they wear on their heads."* And, as it also says in I Timothy 2:9: *"I also want the women to be modest and sensible about their clothes and to dress properly; not with fancy hair styles or with gold ornaments or pearls or expensive dresses."*

- Do not hang framed pictures of any kind in the home.
- Keep plain rugs on the floor, no stripes through them.
- There shall be no flowered oil cloths on the table.
- Dresses are to be worn down to the ankles. No light stockings which show bare legs.
- Fasten dresses and aprons with straight pins only.

---

* As Judas was replaced by "casting of the lot," so do the Amish add or replace a minister. Every married man is eligible to participate in the process. To some this may seem to be nothing more than luck of the draw. But to the Amish it is God's will. When an Amish man is baptized, usually between the ages 18 to 21, the church asks him if he will be a preacher if chosen by lot. If he answers "no" he will not be baptized into church membership.

** Amish ministers must be well educated concerning the *Bible* as they will be required to preach long sermons without using notes of any kind. They must speak freely but never in "tongues" as do some fundamentalist groups.

*** This means that an Amish farmer, for example, is not permitted to place any signs anywhere on his farm advertising a certain animal feed that he uses for his animals, a particular corn seed he may have planted, type of cattle bred on the farm, etc. To do otherwise would show pride and would be considered as grounds for excommunication.

**** In the Amish religion, the home is the "church" where all religious services occur. Thus the Amish home is viewed as a sanctuary, a sacred place.

***** In this particular Amish church, married and unmarried women both wear a full length, neck to ankles apron that is the same color as their plain dress they are wearing on that particular day. However, unmarried girls wear a see through, white organdy **apron on Sundays, at weddings, singings, etc.**

Children and Growing Up

Amish couples do not practice birth control and pray for children. It is indeed a happy occasion when a child is born to Amish parents. A new baby is showered with love and neighbors come from miles around for "sweet coffee." "Sweet coffee" is the term, in the writer's former Amish community, given to the custom of visiting and eating at the home of the grateful Amish parents. There are no Godfather ceremonies nor gifts.

Children are very important in this culture. As my father used to say, "Put the swing where the children want it, the grass will grow back."

In the following letter, an Amish lady best describes the Amish people's feelings concerning birth control.

The Pill

...in these times some may be tempted not to have a family or limit the size. Read Genesis 38:9. The pill, I would say, is not pleasing to God who has made us pure and holy. Paul writes that young women should marry, bear children and guide the house.

Anonymous— Reprinted from *Family Life*

This writer has never known a time when the birth of a child was an unwelcomed event in the Amish community. A baby means another corn husker, another cow-milker, but, most of all, another God-fearing Amishman. The birth is always seen as a blessing of the Lord. Thus, Amish parents feel that their children really do not belong to them. As the Amish mother in the following piece indicates, **"I have no children,"** they belong to God.

I Have No Children

I am a young mother and our house rings with merry voices and childish laughter. However, I have no children. God has given us on loan, two precious souls to nurture and cherish for a period of time to fit them for the Kingdom.

If these were MY children, I would love them so much I could not bear to punish them. I would overlook their childish tantrums and if they should strike me while angry, I would smile indulgently. But because these children belong to the Lord, and I am His servant, I will punish them when necessary. Whom the Lord loveth, He chasteneth, and can His servants do less? Also, because His word warns that children should obey and respect their parents (Eph. 6:1), I will not permit a child to strike at me jokingly, much less in anger.

If these were MY children I would want to dress them attractively to draw attention to the natural beauty which God has blessed them with. However, because these are God's children and His word refers often to the dress of immoral women, (Prov. 7:10), I will dress them modestly when they are small, so that as they reach the age of accountability, they will not be strangers to God's standard of dress. First of all I will hold forth this standards in my own life, (I Tim. 2:9) because God has blessed me with hands to sew and I cannot blame my dress standard on others.

If these children belonged to ME I would want to send them to the best schools, have them read all the current best sellers, regardless of content, and in every way fit them to obtain good jobs and live a life of ease. But since these are God's children, and if the Lord tarries till they are of school age, I will send them to a Christian day school to help fit them for eternity, and trust God to lead them when school years are past.

If these were MY children as they enter their teen years, I would provide them with all the "extras," a car, radio, television and the latest fashionable clothes, so that they would be invited to the best places, date the most prominent people and in general "live it up" before settling down to earn a living. But since these are God's children, I will, with His help, admonish them and teach them by word and by example that God commands us to abstain from the unequal yoke. Also, together we will read and strive to obey Titus, Chapter 2, for this is God's order for our life. At no time will I give the impression that the teen years are for foolishness and seeking pleasure, but rather for seeking God's will for our adult life. I will try to impress upon them that "What a man sows, that must he also reap."

If these were MY children and I followed my own selfish desires for their life I would share with them as much as possible in enjoying the worldly pleasures and in seeking after such. I would also spend with them an endless eternity in the torments of hell and I would be largely responsible as their mother for influencing them in that direction. After it is too late we would see that a life lived for self and things done for the glory of man have their reward in eternal suffering.

However, because these are God's children, and I have renounced self and seek to obey my husband as he obeys God, we, through the grace of God and the keeping power of our Lord Jesus Christ, will share the joys of Heaven throughout the ceaseless ages of eternity, to Him be all honor, praise and glory.

Anonymous—Reprinted from *Family Life*

The Amish are a fertile group and very few couples are without offspring. Families usually range from eight to ten children. There were two Amish families in my community with 15 natural children. Couples without children are a rarity and childless couples often adopt non-Amish babies. The latter has caused consternation among some "local" uninformed outsiders.

———————▶●◀———————

My Baby Brother

Noah was born last Tuesday and our family is excited. We are now a family of 5 boys and 5 girls. Noah is tiny and red but dad says he will grow up to be a good farmer like all my brothers and me....

Yost, fifth grade

———————▶●◀———————

Today more and more Amish children are being delivered in local hospitals; however, most are still delivered at home, as was the writer, by an Amish midwife. Sometimes, as in my case, someone forgets to record the birth with local officials. Thanks to carefully kept records in the family *Bible*, I obtained a valid birth certificate when entering high school.

My contacts with MDs from Amish communities and with Amish mid-wives indicate that Amish women generally have an easy time in having their children. It is unknown where the mid-wife receives her training, but I assume it is through observation. I was never present in the room where children were delivered. However, I remember, on at least one occasion, carrying the boiling water to the entrance of the room where my older sister was delivering. In this case, the midwife, my stepmother and the new mother's husband were the only ones present in the room where the delivery occurred.

Non-Amish people marvel at the attention, the love and the affection given to the newborn infant. Even when asleep the infant will often be in someone's arms. For the first several months of life he or she will be held almost constantly by some member of the family. It is the custom to take the baby with them wherever the parents go, even to the fields to work. And, the baby will also attend the long church services when just a few weeks old.

The Amish baby is a pleasure and a gift of God who is too precious to be left in a nursery or with a baby sitter. A baby is an integral part of the family from the moment of birth. The attention and love given to the baby is difficult to describe; you almost have to observe it to understand its significance.

There may be such a thing as a spoiled baby; however, Amish parents seldom refer to an infant as being spoiled. Matter of fact, an infant can do no wrong, they remain blameless. If adjustment problems occur, the parents and community erred.

As previously mentioned, an Amish baby receives much attention and affection. For example, an Amish baby is not diapered on some cold table. This activity is carried out on someone's lap, usually the mother or an older sister.

Amish parents seldom read the books on how to raise children and they do not stick to strict time schedules and so forth. If a baby cries, something is wrong, and if hungry, he or she is fed regardless of the hour.

Food from the table is shared with the baby at a very early age. It is not unusual to see a four month-old baby being fed mashed potatoes directly from the table while sitting in the mother's lap. Eating is a very important activity for an Amish family and they feel that one always eats better in a group. Eating is a family affair which includes the baby.

To an outsider it may appear that the Amish mother is hiding her infant from the eyes of the world when she is in public. The baby is almost always covered in its entirety with a blanket. Amish women always wear a black shawl over their shoulders and many times it is almost impossible to realize that the mother is carrying a baby. She will have the baby carefully tucked away under her shawl. I once asked a late aunt about this custom and she indicated that the Amish child should be protected, at an early age, from the "world."

Every Amish baby, if physically possible, is breast fed. I do not feel that any turmoil exists in the Amish culture concerning whether to breast feed or not to. It is simply the only thing to do. Breasts are not seen as sex symbols and feeding may take place anywhere at any time, as no apparent shame or humility is attached to breast feeding in public. This should not be construed to mean that breast feeding will take place in a local department store. However, when Amish are gathered socially, or in church, breast feeding takes place without any apparent shame. As the following Amish lady's letter indicates, it is seen as being very natural.

Breast Feeding

...I am a believer in nature as part of God's creation. The plain people are becoming somewhat indifferent as to what used to be the rule for mothers in the past. In Lamentations 2:3 we can read, "The daughter of my people is become cruel, like the ostriches in the wilderness." I have heard that the hen ostrich cares very little for her nest or her offspring. The male cares for them nights which is quite the reverse for most all other creatures.

"The tongue of the sucking child cleaveth to the roof of his mouth for thirst" (Lam. 4:4). I once read a doctor's article that dealt close to nature. He remarked that the invention of the bottle has been the greatest single cause of colic.

Man is also given an example in nature. Even the sea monsters draw out the breast. They give suck to their young ones. (This is their life).

This is not meant to offend anyone, but it says not "my people" but "the daughter of my people." It may seem incorrect to say, "Thy will be done" when no effort is made to use members in the way God intended.

Anonymous—Reprinted from *Family Life*

Another aspect of Amish child rearing which is uncommon to the "outsider" culture is the fact that the new baby often sleeps with his or her parents for the first few months of life. Along with the security this practice affords, it is also convenient for breast feeding and provides warmth. Psychologically, this practice may contribute more to the Amish youths' apparent security than any other factor. It is difficult to pinpoint the age at which weaning occurs. However, contrary to medical fact, many Amish still believe that the longer they nurse the less is the chance of another pregnancy and thus Amish babies usually nurse longer than babies of the "outsider" culture. Breast feeding is viewed as a natural form of birth control.

Toilet training usually begins around age two with no apparent harshness or anxiety attached to the endeavor. As previously stated, Amish babies are held almost constantly, and of course, in the absence of rubber pants or snap on diapers (which are considered "worldly") they often leave their "mark" on the holder's lap. This may draw a snicker from an "outsider" observer; however, the wet spot warrants no attention or concern from the Amish people present. In the absence of modern, closed-in bathrooms, waste containers for human elimination (these are usually gray or white porcelain) are evident in Amish bedrooms. To the Amish, human elimination is simply a natural activity and thus toilet training is facilitated by the process of imitation and observation. This should not be construed to mean that there is no privacy; however, there is much less concern over privacy associated with this endeavor than in the "outsider" culture. Bedroom doors are not fitted with locks.

Amish parents believe that one of their basic duties is to transmit the Amish cultural heritage to their children. They are not alone in this high priority activity as the total Amish community is highly involved in the rearing of all its participants. However, as in any culture, child rearing is not taken lightly. Some Amish parents provide some rules for raising children in the following essay written for *Family Life*.

Things To Do BEFORE Your Children Grow Up

Train up a child in the way he should go, and when he is old, he will not depart from it (Proverbs 22:6).

"These words, which I command thee shall be in thine heart and thou shalt teach them diligently unto thy children, and shalt talk of them when thou sittest in thine house and when thou walkest by the way and when thou liest down, and when thou risest up" (Deut. 22:5-6)

We must be by example what we want our children to be. Children are great imitators. Your example is of utmost importance.

Be a parent, not just a playmate, but do play and pray together. If you love your children, then let *idleness* be counted as a sin in your family.

Be sure you have confidence in your children and they in you.

Let them know you are for them and not against them.

Be as good as your word if you want them to be as good as their word.

Work along with your children in their work and take an interest in what they do, or they may lose interest in what they do.

Pray for your children. The genuineness of your prayers will teach them the reality of God.

Devotions should not be merely an instruction period, but rather adoration, praise, love and appreciation of God.

Songs of praise magnify the wonders of God.

When conditions are as they should be in the home, it is a foretaste of Heaven.

As fathers and mothers, grandfathers and grandmothers, we have the biggest job in the world to teach our children to love the Lord.

Disobedience and disrespect for parents are often the first steps downward that children take.

No man who dishonors father or mother ever prospers in the long run.

Isaac was so holy before his children, that when Jacob remembered God, he remembered him in the "fear of his father Isaac" (Gen. 31:53).

When parents err in their judgment and later recognize and confess it, they gain the respect of the child.

Unity between parents is a must. When one parent says something, the other should back him up.

Study your *Bible*: acquaint your children with the simple truths of the Word.

There must be much gentleness and patience along

with instructions, "lest they become discouraged" (Col. 3:21).

It always pays to speak kindly, and especially to husband, wife or children.

If parents want the gratitude of their children, let them talk to them as though they were human beings. "Like begets like."

Love produces love and hatred reproduces hatred. It is usually the scolding parents who are disrespected by their children. Reproofs should always be given in gentle tones.

These do not belong in a Christian home: slang, vulgarity, frivolity, uncourteous treatment of youngsters, disrespect for elders, talking back to parents.

Never compare your child with other children. If you compare them favorably, they may become proud, if unfavorably, discouraged.

As soon as children show anger, they are old enough to be punished. A child will not desire to touch a hot stove more than once or twice. Our discipline should follow the same pattern.

A child is not trained properly until he obeys when told the first time, without question, and without need for the parent to raise his voice.

Use discipline to correct your child, be fair but be firm.

Mother shall help faithfully, but Father must shoulder the blame if training of the children is not accomplished.

If the woman has the lead in the conversation too much in the home, it is evidence that she is out of God's order: Christ, man, and then woman.

In the sight of God it is much better for the woman to be of a meek and quiet spirit (I Peter 3:3-4).

Demanding obedience to satisfy every selfish whim or acting like a slave driver without due respect for the children, cannot be tolerated in the Christian home. Children will quickly discern whether or not we mean what we say.

When children are old enough to understand, they should be taught the basic facts about sex and the reproduction of life before they learn it from a perverted source in an unscriptural manner.

Young people may develop sinful habits because they are not aware of the meaning of the impulses within them. A knowledge of the facts of life can help them from getting into habits which may trouble them for life.

Buying everything he wants results in a spoiled child. The parents should know what is best for the children.

When our children leave for school and other places, do we send them off with a smile and a pleasant farewell?

A child can read a parent's character before he can read the alphabet.

You can't pull the wool over the children's eyes so the best way to teach the Gospel is to live it.

When childhood closes, life's training is mostly done.

Children have only one childhood. We can fail in business and often times start over and make good. But if we fail in the teaching and training of our children, we never get another chance.

To be really effective in training up a child in the way he should go, we must be sure that we travel that road ourselves first.

— Compiled by Amish parents who have a concern for the on-coming generation.

Anonymous—Reprinted from *Family Life*

At approximately the age of two, restrictions and exacting disciplines have already begun to be continually imposed on the

Amish child. Amish parents inform their children at a very young age why they cannot have store-bought "worldly" clothes, bicycles and other type toys like those of the children who live outside the Amish community. They are given sound Biblical reasons as to why their family cannot have electricity, cars, radios, televisions and comic books. Amish children are taught that they should remain separate and different from the strange and fearful "outsider" world.

Amish children are taught to speak in German and Amish parents do not want anyone speaking English to their infants. The learning of English comes at a later time; just previous to entering the first grade. A four- or five-year-old Amish child seldom understands or speaks English.

Amish youth are taught respect for those in authority. They will learn to enjoy work and to fulfill their responsibilities. The obedience expected from Amish children is not based on strict authority but instead is based on love and the belief that those in authority truly have the concern for them. By this I mean that you soon learn that those in authority care about what happens to you more than they care about themselves. Thus, if your parents have taught you right from wrong, to do wrong would be to let them down and show your lack of concern for their feelings. You learn through a gradual process of indoctrination to be truly concerned with the feelings of those around you and especially the feelings of those in authority. This brings about humbleness and guilt feelings when you let these people down by doing "wrong." Although the "outsider" may view this method of child rearing as being harsh, this writer can remember only one "light" physical punishment during his entire time at home. My father used to indicate that the guilt over the concern of hurting others was enough punishment. There may be considerable variation among the Amish communities as to how disobedience is handled. However, it is my estimation that there are fewer physical confrontations between the youth and those in authority than one is led to believe.

The rights of the Amish parents over the children are great. It can be observed that Amish children obey and respect their parents and very little of the children's behavior is irrelevant to the parents, especially their father. He feels justified in observing the Biblical right to influence most of their actions. It is evident that the Amish wife and children are submissive to him, but his values tell the Amish father that he has the cultural and Biblical responsibility to run the family. The Amish father does initiate the action in the family, but the rarity of arbitrary decisions on his part is impressive.

Some "outsiders" may feel that the value orientation patterns prescribed for the Amish children will accomplish social conformity at the expense of curiosity and fantasies about the "real world." This is the desire of Amish parents. And, in the absence of newspapers, books, fairy tales, radio, television and creative surroundings, the Amish youth's imagination and creativity are at a minimum. Yet, Amish youth appear to be happy and satisfied with their life as it is and feel very insecure when away from home and community.

Much emphasis is placed on teaching the young Amish child the value of sharing. If there is a smaller baby or infant the pre-schooler will be taught how to care for the child; helping to tie shoes and so forth. Older children can often be observed in helping their younger siblings put on shoes, coats, boots and other articles of clothing. Although the younger child may be able to accomplish these tasks alone, he or she may wait for the assistance of an older sibling. My late father (as do other Amish) felt that being given the opportunity to help someone you cared for strengthened the bond between you.

Two Special Sisters

I like to help my mother in the house. I help her take care of my two little sisters. They are on a special diet. They can't have cake or pie, just special cookies. They can only have potatoes, green beans and some other vegetables, but not many of them. All their food has to be weighed. They are not allowed to have flour, milk or eggs. We bake some cookies with a special wheat starch, and use artificial milk for their cereal, which must also be in small amounts and weighed.

My one sister cannot help herself very well, but she can talk and is very pleasant to care for.

I have other sisters, too. We all help each other care for our little sisters. There is always plenty of

work to do.

I am thankful for the many blessings we have.

Grade 5, Age 11, Reprinted from *Family Life*

———————●————————

Amish parents believe that a young child does not know the difference between right and wrong. The child was born without sin and is blameless. Thus, it is their duty to teach their children the difference between right and wrong so that they will choose the correct way of the Amish culture. Temper tantrums, making faces, name calling and so forth among Amish youngsters are extremely rare. Amish children are taught humility and to obey. This can readily be observed at the table as Amish youth speak only when spoken to. Fighting and quarreling among siblings and peers is at a minimum. As mentioned above, sibling members learn to share and it is common to see several brothers and sisters eating from the same school lunch bucket at an Amish parochial school. There is very little conflict among Amish family members. Amish youngsters are taught to settle their differences by talking to the person with whom they differ. Should two adult Amishmen come into conflict, both bring two other Amishmen with them to a meeting where the six settle the differences. Amish youngsters learn to imitate their parents and do not observe cowboys on television settling their differences with guns!

Amish children do not receive an allowance. Should the parents take a child along to town, he or she may be given a small sum of money with which to buy candy. It is strictly taboo to spend money on Sunday and in any manner for individual recreation. However, sometimes a family will visit a zoo or a similar place. Should some of the sons or daughters "hire out" for a few days, any money earned by them would automatically be turned over to their father. This continues until the youth reaches the age of 21 or marries, whichever comes first. The Amish family is often described as an economic model that teaches its children thriftiness. Amish fathers are known to be *extremely* parsimonious. This value pattern is transmitted from parents to offspring by imitation and observation.

Special significance to family interaction and value patterns can be observed at the family table. The whole family gathers here three times a day for family discussions and spiritual devotion. During the family meals the value patterns of the family and community are overtly evident. A meal is not eaten without all existing family members being present; and lateness to the table is not tolerated. Each family member has an assigned seating place at the table. This place at the table becomes symbolic of belonging to the family and is evidence of family solidarity. When this place is vacated by death, by marriage, by father having gone to town or by discipline of the *Meidung*, it becomes a subject of deep concern.

Silent prayers are said before and after the meal. No one excuses him or herself from the table until the final silent prayer is observed. To memorize and recite a prayer would be evidence of self pride and would be contrary to the prescribed value of humility. (All family prayers, during morning and evening devotional periods, are read from prayer books. Reading occurs even though it is obvious that the father, down through the years, has memorized the prayer. The same prayer is read each devotional period. The entire family is on its knees in unison.)

As noted, children are a gift from God and are a special treasure. There is an Amish saying that goes something like this: *"Place the swing where the children want it as the grass will always grow back"* which clearly reveals the importance of children. Another Amish saying concerning children is as follows: *Always treat children in the direction you wish them to grow, not as they now are.* However, although they are often pampered, Amish children are also given strict obedience training early in life.

An important aspect of obedience training is how children should respond during prayer time. That is, to the Amish, it is very important that Amish infants and toddlers learn to appropriately fold their hands in their laps during prayers. I have personally observed many an Amish toddler being held in someone's lap at the table and their little hands enclosed in the adult's larger tightly folded hands during the silent grace before and after the meal.

Learning to pray correctly, along with being quiet in church, is very important for even a very young child to learn. Thus, putting a child's hands together and down in their laps (never up in the air as this is the way members of the world pray) for every prayer is taught very early in life. Adults stay at it until the child learns to obey this very important command.

Talking at the table is not encouraged for the sake of conversation. Mealtime becomes the time for expressing likes and dislikes, discussing the prescribed values of the family and community, discussing work to be done and decision making.

The Amish believe their actions to be more important than their reflections or thinking. This can best be observed by the parents' lack of teaching the "outsiders'" common courtesies of "pardon me" and so forth to their children. An Amishman's loud "belch" following dinner is more of an indication to the cook that he enjoyed the meal than saying "thank you." It is seldom that anyone asks another to pass the food that he himself can reach, everyone reaches and helps himself in an orderly manner. It is a tradition, following the pre-meal prayers, for the Amish father to state, "Reach and help yourself." It is also uncommon for an Amishman to knock on another Amishman's door before entering his home. And dinner guests often drop in at the last minute without a previous invitation. They teach that actions of kindness are much more important than mere words or money. This was in evidence several years ago when several bus loads of adult males from an Amish community in Pennsylvania traveled to Mississippi at their own expense to assist non-Amish following hurricane Camile. Also, the Amish farmer does not believe in the "outsider's" method of "social security" and is exempt from paying it. He knows his neighbors will be there when he needs them. And they do not send money to feed the poor in India, for example, they will have a community "butchering" and send several thousand cans of "home-canned" beef or pork. When Amish gather in mass to help someone it is called a "frolic" and almost always ends with homemade ice cream for all. A ten-year-old Amish boy writes about such a "frolic" in the following essay in the *Blackboard Bulletin*.

A Field of Corn

Last spring the parents of our school decided to plant a field of corn. It was a 17-acre field, and the corn was planted to help pay for our schoolhouse. One day a frolic was made to plow the field. They had the plowing done in one day. Then the parents of the school planted the corn and took care of it.

Then on October 28, another frolic was held in this corn field. The men, women and children got together to help husk the corn. Some of the women made dinner.

The husking was done by 4:00. We had ice cream in the afternoon.

Grade 4, Age 10

Anonymous—Reprinted from the *Blackboard Bulletin*

Family group participation in recreation is at a minimum. As previously stated, spending money for any type of recreation is strictly taboo. This includes the purchase of any type of recreational equipment for the home and any forms of enjoyment for the family must be home-made and simple. Young girls find pleasure in clapping games while boys enjoy playing with a home-made checker set or going hunting. Weekly auctions, a favorite pastime, or visiting relatives, eating supper with friends, threshing meetings, husking bees, barn raisings, frolics of all sorts and weddings take up much of the leisure time of both children and adults.

The home is extremely important to the Amish family. It is in the home where you are born, go to church, get married and where your funeral will be held. In the essay below, an Old Order Amish person writes about the home and the importance of keeping it simple. As with most short essays in *Family Life*, this one is unsigned, but it is definitely a female writer and, I feel that the reader will agree that she paints a beautiful picture of the simple Amish family life.

I Am Rich

Home is a place to relax. It need not be a fancy structure or modern. It is not just a place to eat and sleep and change clothes like a filling station. It can be a harbor of peace—if the Lord is permitted inside.

In our home we have no running water. A pump at the kitchen sink furnishes all the water we care to use. We have no skin problems for with our silky rain water, we need no detergents. When getting dinner for company, we never have to stop and run to the basement, because the pressure is way down. There is very little expense involved with our water system, just an occasional change of leather and that requires no mechanical ability. As for hot water, we have our old reliable teakettle. For heating wash water we use the iron kettle and feel it is a luxury because in many parts of the world the people do their laundry in the creeks.

Heating? We have no central heating system, not even an enameled stove. All we have is the same black model which for many is only a childhood memory. When coming inside, how comfortable to warm our chilling fingers. Where else could we toast our feet so satisfactorily and feel the warmth seep upward through the veins? Of course it must be fed and in zero or subzero temperatures, it's a starving creature. But with the basement filled with wood, which the members of our family have labored so generously to provide for us, what more could we ask? When I look at the ricks of wood, I feel humbly grateful for I know that in the world, many people are cold, living in huts, without even a blanket.

We have no padded or overstuffed seats to sit down upon. All we have are the lightweight hickory rockers and they are so portable. If we need more light we carry one to the window, if we're cold we carry it to the stove and prop up our feet in a very un-lady-like manner on the nickel trimmings of our stove. If someone comes with a baby, the rocker can be moved to the bedroom for there it is quiet. When it comes to entertainment we have the very best. Mother Nature is our

Master Performer—the beauty of bare branches etched in front of a colorful sunset. I wonder how many people ever notice the varying branch formations on different trees. The cool colors of a winter sunrise are often overlooked by sleepy eyes. The ever-changing sky always has something interesting to see. The fluffy clouds of summer, the turbulence of a windy day in spring, or a heavy snowfall in winter, each season has its attractions.

In our leisure time we often watch our little feathered friends. It is a thrifty form of entertainment with a home-made bird feeder, homegrown sunflower and squash seeds and corn. How exciting to see our first evening grosbeak! The pileated woodpecker may be as homely as a mudpie but it is still a rare sight to behold. The saucy chickadee darts between the suet and feeder, almost faster than the eye can see. Even some kinds of our lowly sparrows are very attractive.

For real excitement on the farm, there's nothing like gathering in the first eggs from a flock of chickens you've raised from baby chicks. Nor is there anything as tasty as vegetables you've hoed and cultivated till you're hot and tired. When we stop to consider, it's nothing short of a miracle when we behold how much God provides for us to eat, all from one little dried-up dead-looking seed.

No, we have no so-called modern conveniences, but we are blessed with an abundance of life's necessities. We don't have an over-flowing grocery cart, or beautiful clothes or a big bank account to fall back on.

But I do have a family and friends, and many people I meet on life's highway. I have good eyesight, a healthy mind and body. I AM RICH.

May I remember to be as rich with gratitude as I am rich with gifts which God has bestowed upon me.

Anonymous—Reprinted from *Family Life*

Much of the Amish educational process takes place at home. Amish parents feel that their children belong to them rather than to the state and that it is their obligation to educate them in the totality of the growing up process. All Amish adults are models in this educational process. However, the chief adult models of the Amish culture are the farmer and the housewife. The Amish religion is most compatible with farming and it is understood that children will some day farm or be a farmer's wife. Both boys and girls are given farming-related responsibilities around the ages of four and five. Four- and five-year-olds can be seen pumping water by hand and are also taught how to milk cows and do other farm related chores. Amish boys will be doing field work with horses by the time they are six or seven years old. I remember when six, my father put me on a two-horse, single-row, corn cultivator and I started down the corn row. I had not yet learned how to turn the horses around at the end of the field and head them back the other direction. Therefore, my older brother, just one corn row over with his horses, reached the end of the field at approximately the same time as I, turned my horses around and sent us back the other direction. This process continued until I learned to turn my team alone. Also, at a very young age I had certain cows assigned to me for milking both night and morning. Our 20 plus cows all had Amish-type names and the ones assigned to me at that age were gentle ones.

An Amish child learns early in life that work is a moral directive. Amish people generally rise around 4:30 or 5:00 in the morning. The lanterns are lit and they go to the barn to milk the cows and do the other farm-related activities. It is true that Amish youngsters work hard, but in actuality, pleasure becomes associated with work.

A Ride to Town

I really like the long buggy rides to town with my Dad. Children in my family take turns going with Dad to town and it is a treat to be the one chosen to go. Some Amish hire an outsider driver and like to go to town with the car. But I like to go in our buggy. A trip to town takes all day and gives plenty of time for talking with neighbors and relatives on the way to town and back home. We are never in a hurry and often stop to chat with neighbors along the way. My Dad always says, "What's the hurry anyway?" Dad says you can't be in a rush in a buggy and that it is a lot more calm and enjoyable than riding in a car and I agree. Dad says you can see the real beauty of God's earth while riding slowly along in buggy. I'm looking forward to my next trip to town with Dad.

Silas, eighth grade

————————●◄————————

People often ask about the Amish parental method of teaching their children about sex. Actually, there is very little teaching by the parents. Yet, in my opinion, the Amish may have one of the more healthy outlooks regarding sex of any cultural group known. Perhaps some things are better left not said than to be communicated in a confusing and insincere manner. However, although not necessarily encouraged to do so, Amish children observe the sexual acts of farm animals and are often present at animal births. Their notions and emotions, regarding sex, are not contaminated by television, movies and otherwise as is often the case in the turbulent culture that surrounds these children. An Amish male has an eye for female beauty; however, her beauty is not camouflaged by make-up and perfume, and her weight is not a factor. The Amish youths' feelings regarding sex spring naturally from their surroundings. And, sexual deviates and perverts are unknown to Amish communities. I have no knowledge of an Amish homosexual or "gay" and have never heard the term, or its equivalent, used by an Amish person to describe another Amish individual's sexual preference.

It is evident from the essays and letters appearing in this section that the Amish are truly a hardworking, peace-loving sect. They are very humble people and children are taught this value early in life. And, the home, the church and the school all teach the same values. Amish youngsters are taught to fill their places in the little community as it has been planned for them; they are not taught individuality nor how to make their place in the "world." They are taught the values of honesty, thrift, love and purity. These values, lived by Amish adults, gain their children's allegiance. And, Amish children are not exposed to books, television shows nor movies that teach opposing values. Thus, they live what they learn and learn what they live.

Some social scientists have long stated that mankind has an innate, violent and aggressive nature. The more than 175,000 Old Order Amish people contradict this. Humility, as well as violence (like strapping big guns on little boys, my dad used to say), can be taught, according to the Amish parents.

Mounting evidence indicates that the Amish maintain one of the strongest and most stable family systems in America. This is due, in part, to the peaceable, slow-paced, stress free lifestyle they live. In addition, among the benefits of being Amish is having a guaranteed built-in-social identity and a ready-made support system for every Amish individual. Amish children face little uncertainly regarding their future vocation or the role they will play within the community as their life is structured and the future is set. Research indicates that living within a culture that provides such a well-defined social identity and support system is of great value to its participants, both psychologically and physically. For example, researchers have provided data indicating that major depression occurs about one fifth to one tenth as often among Old Order Amish individuals as it does among the rest of the US population. In addition, the Harvard School of Medicine's recent findings revealed that Amish people have a much lower rate of heart disease than do average Americans. Many more such benefits could be given for living a stress free, slow-paced Amish lifestyle. However, Amish life is not all positive and most certainly is not "Camelot." However, one can understand why approximately 85% of their children grow up to become lifetime members of the Amish church.

Section IV

Rules for Living

The Orders of the Church

Throughout this book reference has been made to specific details that may not be applicable to all Old Order Amish church districts. Each district has its own unique *Ordnung* or Church Orders. For example, there was a small Orange County, Indiana Amish settlement where males began their beards when baptized into the church. However, as mentioned previously, in my former community none of the six church districts require the male to grow a beard until marriage. It should be acknowledged that this Orange County Amish group ran into extreme difficulties with the Indiana law requiring the orange, slow moving vehicle (SMV) emblem to be affixed to their buggies. Several were jailed for refusing to affix the sign to their buggies. Finally, the entire community emigrated to South America in search of religious freedom.

Church districts within each Amish community are formed geographically in such a manner so as to consist of around 30-35 families each. An Amish family may cross districts to attend church, especially if services of another district are being held in a close relative's home. However, if a family attends another district's service, they must abide, if at all possible, by that church's *Ordnung* for that particular Sunday.

Amish church *Ordnung* are almost never put into writing. I wrote several Amish ministers requesting copies of their church's *Ordnung* and had several responses indicating that none existed (in writing) for their church. Thus, I was surprised to receive the following from an Old Order Amish minister from a midwestern state. He wrote in part, **"This is close to what we follow here in _____, but we don't give copies to the members. Please** *don't use my* **name or district."**

I think the reader will agree that it would take a lot of self-discipline and a true belief in God to follow such firm and strict "orders" in the twenty-first century!

Church Ordinances

No ornamental, bright, showy form-fitting, immodest or silk-like clothing of any kind. Colors such as bright red, orange, yellow and pink not allowed. Amish form of clothing to be followed as a general rule. Costly Sunday clothes to be discouraged. Dresses not shorter than halfway between knees and floor, nor over eight inches from floor. Longer advisable. Clothing in every way modest, serviceable and as simple as scripturally possible. Only outside pockets allowed on work *oberhem* **(pants) or** *voma* **(coat) and pockets on large overcoats. Dress shoes, if any, to be plain and black only. No high heels and pomp slippers. Dress socks, if any, to be black except white for foot hygiene for both sexes. A plain, unshowy suspender without buckles (males of all ages must wear suspenders).**

Hat to be black with no less than 3-inch brim and not extremely high in crown. No stylish impressions in any hat. No pressed trousers. No sweaters.

Prayer covering to be simple, and made to fit head. Should cover all the hair as nearly as possible and is to be worn wherever possible. Pleating of caps to be discouraged. No silk ribbons.

Young children to dress according to the Word as well as parents. No pink or fancy baby blankets or caps.

Women to wear shawls, bonnets and capes in public. Aprons to be worn at all times. No adorning of hair among either sex such as parting of hair among men and curling or waving among women.

A full beard should be worn among men and boys before baptism if possible. No shingled hair. Length at least halfway below top of ears.

No decorations of any kind in buildings inside or out. No fancy yard fences. Linoleum, oilcloth, shelf and wall paper to be plain and unshowy. Overstuffed furniture or any luxury items forbidden. No doilies or napkins. No large mirrors, fancy glassware, statues or wall pictures for decorations.

No embroidery work of any kind. Curtains either dark green rollers or black cloth. No boughten dolls.

No bottle gas or high line electrical appliances.

Stoves should be black if bought new.

Weddings should be simple and without decorations. Names not attached to gifts.

No ornaments on buggies or harness.

Tractors to be used only for such things that can hardly be done with horses. Only either stationary engines or tractors with steel tires allowed. No air-filled rubber tires.

Farming and related occupations to be encouraged. Working in cities or factories not permissible. Boys and girls working out away from home for world people forbidden except in emergencies.

Worldly amusements as radios, card playing, party games, movies, fairs, etc. forbidden. Reading, singing, *Bible* games, relief work, giving of tithes, etc. are encouraged.

Musical instruments or different voice singing not permissible. No dirty, silly talking or sex teasing of children.

Usury (interest) forbidden in most instances. No government benefit payments or partnership in harmful associations. No insurance. No photographs.

No buying or selling of anything on Sunday. It should be kept according to the principles of the Sabbath. Worship of some kind every Sunday.

Women should spend time in doing good or reading God's Word instead of taking care of canaries, goldfish or house flowers.

Church confession is to be made if practical where transgression was made. If not, a written request of forgiveness should be made to said church. All manifest sins to be openly confessed before church before being allowed to commune. I Tim. 5:20. A period of time required before taking new members into full fellowship.

Because of a great falling away from sound doctrine, we do not care to fellowship, that is hold communion, with any churches that allow or uphold any unfruitful works of darkness such as worldliness, fashionable attire, bed-courtship, habitual smoking or drinking, old wives fables, non-assurance of salvation, anti-missionary zeal or anything contrary to sound doctrine.

Ordnung Reasons

Because the *Bible* does not specify a certain mode of dress, some people seem to think the church does not have the right to say what we should wear. But let us not forget that neither does the word of God in a specific way say that infant baptism is wrong, yet our forefathers were willing to give their lives rather than practice it. Neither is specific mention made of gambling, movies, radios, bed-courtship, etc., yet we believe they are wrong.

Webster's definition of luxury is the free indulgence in food and liquor, dress or equipage. Living in luxury is condemned. Having costly modern machinery, furniture, an auto, electricity, etc. would also come into that class.

To have all these things a person usually has to invest much money that might well be used otherwise. It can also cause people to go into debt deeper. Those with tractors usually farm more land, sometimes taking it away from poor people.

Following certain rules regarding suspenders, window curtains, clothing, etc. does not mean that any church having any different rules regarding these items is necessarily wrong. We believe it is the right and the duty of our church to observe any restrictions that would help to keep its members from being tempted so much to buy or wear fashionable clothes or to be found in places of worldly amusements, etc.

Take, for example, window curtains. We have no doubt that the two kinds mentioned are sufficient and also scriptural and do not give an appearance of decorations. But that is not saying that churches having other curtains are wrong provided they are plain. But any lace, fancy or showy curtain is wrong anywhere.

As to buckle suspenders, we do not believe they violate any scripture if they can be had strictly plain. But as plain ones are oftimes hard to get and oftimes those that are bought are not plain, we believe it would be better to use the others.

From what the old testament says about the beard... it is evident that it was considered a shame for a man to be without a beard and that full beard was worn. And why should we now be ashamed to look as God created us if He created us in His image? ...So if we change the image in which we were created, doesn't it look as if we were not satisfied with the way God created us?

As to the length of hair, if we stop to look how we are created, hair on the head grows out profusely perhaps a little over halfway below the top of the ears. We have scripture that we shall not wear them long like woman, therefore it appears the above length would be having them as God intended.... Furthermore, there are not two sets of rules given for members of the church, so if it is necessary to wear a beard upon marriage, it is also necessary on baptism.

Jesus said the world hates Him because He testifies that its works are evil. Therefore if we testify that it is wrong to do unnecessary work on Sunday as we believe it is to pick up milk and take care of it on Sunday, and at the same time would be a cause of them picking it up and taking care of it, would this be consistent?

The foregoing ordinances are considered the nearest scriptural under present day conditions, but should not be considered unchangeable, as different circumstances may require different regulations.

There could much more be written but to explain everything in detail would require several books. We hope everyone who reads this will be willing to live up to the enlightenment he has and also realize that no person or church is perfect for our knowledge is only in part.

Therefore should anyone find anything they consider unscriptural, we hope they will show Christian charity towards us and not remain silent. We hope, with God's help, to be ready to be admonished at any time, if in harmony with the Word.

Personal correspondence

Writer wishes to remain anonymous

Footwashing

The Amish are one of the few remaining sects, if not the only one, who still practice footwashing. This occurs during communion services twice each year. When the bishop indicates that it is time for this part of the communion service, the deacons and helpers carry in several buckets of lukewarm water and the foot washing begins. The sexes remain separate in this activity. When a same-sex pair completes this activity, they kiss one another on the cheek and "give alms" (money) to the poor. The church orders in several Amish communities require one person washing another person's feet to remain in a "stooped" position. However, in my community, one is permitted to kneel. This may seem trivial to the reader, but not to the Amish. If your church orders indicate that the washer should remain "stooped" so be it! To do otherwise would be viewed as breaking church orders and would not be tolerated. As the following Amish person writes, which position to use is taken very seriously.

Amish church members, those who have been baptized (and are in good standing) practice footwashing twice a year. The church orders in several Amish communities require the person washing the other person's feet to remain in a "stooped" position. However, in my former community, one is permitted to kneel.

The Most Humble Position?

I am wondering what others think on the subject of feet washing. Is there one acceptable way to wash the other brother or sister's feet? Some people think you must bend over your back with straight knees so as to be in subjection to the other person.

It seems to me, if there ever was a time that it should be left up to the individual person as to what seems to him the proper position to do something, it should be in this. When a woman bends over (even if she has on a long dress) her dress goes up. I feel kneeling can be just as lowly as then your whole body is brought low. All through the *Bible* we read that God looketh on the heart, and not on the outward appearance of things. Who is qualified to tell the other man what is the lowliest or most humble way?

Anonymous—Reprinted from *Family Life*

Symbolism of Dress

It is difficult to distinguish that which is and is not religion in the Amish community. Religion is a seven-day-a-week affair, and everything one does and, especially the manner in which one dresses, is based upon religion. When one Amish person sees another, the clothing is recognized as having religious significance.

An Amish woman's hair is never cut and they are not seen publicly with their hair hanging loosely. My own stepmother's hair hung well below her waist. However, only members of her family ever saw her with her hair unbraided. I can only remember a few rare occasions. And, she always had her head covered, usually with the prayer veiling.

The women's prayer veiling or head covering is extremely important in Amish dress. A woman seen without her veiling on her head is considered a sinner. My stepmother even wore her covering to bed with the explanation that she may awaken at night and wish to pray. A young Amish girl writes:

My Covering

The *Bible* says that it is a shame for a girl to have her head uncovered and I think even little girls should wear it to school.

Mom says the covering should cover half your ears and always be tied under your chin. I always wear mine to school....

Esther, fourth grade

Although Amish people would be the last to say that their clothes will take them to heaven, they do believe, as does the Amish lady who wrote the following letter to the *Family Life*, that their clothing is often a protection against **"worldly"** influences and dangers.

The Power of the Covering

I appreciated the article on the covering. Although I have known it is an ordinance of God, yet the article did help to clarify the point for me.

It reminded me of an incident which happened some time ago. My daughter and I were waiting at a bus depot and decided to walk around the block to pass the time. We saw a bookstore across the street as we wanted to see whether they had anything of interest.

As we started down the small flight of stairs, one of the men came outside to meet us. "I'm very sorry," he said, "but women aren't allowed in here."

He seemed to be very courteous and friendly and visited with us awhile, asking whether we are from Pennsylvania, and so forth.

Of course I was greatly surprised to be turned away from a bookstore, but after a hasty glance into the show window I knew the reason and was glad to leave.

It seems strange that someone who will put pornographic literature on display for the public can feel shame to have his merchandise seen by someone he takes for a Christian. His actions showed that he knew better than he was doing.

I feel that we have at times been protected from annoyance, humiliation or worse because of our covering and plain clothes. Only God knows, yet there are so many people who are ashamed to wear them.

Anonymous—Reprinted from *Family Life*

Amish people always speak of dressing modestly. To dress modestly, especially for a female, is to have only the skin of her hands and face uncovered. Also, dressing modestly means wearing loose-fitting dresses, covered entirely with a loose-fitting cape so, as the following teenager writes, **"not to show body form and attract the opposite sex to self."**

Wearing Capes

If mothers expect their daughters to realize why they have to wear the cape dress, then the mothers will have to do their part first. They must see to it that their little girls wear aprons on their dresses in their young years. If Mother doesn't make the apron and prefers to have her little dresses done up in trimmings or puffed out, how can she expect her girls to wear the cape dress when they are grown? She must teach the meaning to it. These things start when the children are small. If Mother changes patterns it will be planted in the children to do likewise. She must teach the meaning, too. First, so as to be separate from the world. Second, so to be modest, not to show body form and attract the opposite sex to self.

Anonymous—Reprinted from *Family Life*

The Amish people also dress modestly to be **"chaste, decent and unpretentious"** and to help boys **"keep their thoughts and actions pure from fleshly lusts."**

More than Tradition

It has long been the practice among our plain churches for the women to wear a cape. But the reason for wearing it is being questioned, and I have even heard of mothers who could not explain why we wear a cape. Some think the cape is an unnecessary article, a hangover of tradition. But let's not miss the point so far. What we do should be scriptural. In I Timothy 2:9 we read, "...that women adorn themselves in modest apparel...."

Now the word modest is defined as chaste, decent and unpretentious. Unpretentious means not showy, or no unnecessary show. But without a cape (or with a fitted cape) we make an unnecessary show of our figure. Young girls may not realize what a struggle boys have to keep their thoughts and actions pure from "fleshly lusts" which I Peter 2:11 exhorts to abstain from. The whole *Bible* teaches that the lusts of the people corrupt a nation. We should learn to help each other. If we sisters by our immodest dress hinder others from thinking pure and holy thoughts we are helping them go the wrong direction.

Anonymous—Reprinted from *Family Life*

Amish people realize their dress is peculiar to the outside world. And, like the young Amish lady who wrote the following, they may have thoughts of dressing **"like the world,"** but, in the long run they're happy to dress differently.

It Does Make a Difference

It was a warm sticky summer evening when I went to a nearby shopping center to do some shopping. I was wearing what I thought was a long dress and I am ashamed to confess that there was a wee bit of envy and resentment in my heart when I saw the other girls and women in the store wearing cool shorts, halters and mini-skirts. Why do I always have to look so different and wear such clothing in this kind of weather, I thought? There is probably no one in this whole store that doesn't think I'd be smarter to dress a little cooler. It probably doesn't mean a thing to anybody in here that I dress this way except to think I'm dumb.

As I walked along, I heard a voice behind me, "Say, it sure is nice to see a young girl dressed decently," a man was talking and he was in earnest. "When you see all these women wearing barely anything, it almost makes you sick." With that he turned and walked away. I was left with a warm glow around my heart and a changed outlook. I decided that if it meant something to him, it probably does to a lot more people. No longer did I resent looking different for I was glad I could.

Anonymous—Reprinted from *Family Life*

As previously mentioned, Amish women believe they should never dress so as to "attract" a male. In the following short essay, a distressed Amish mother writes to an unknown Amish girl (or perhaps a Mennonite) who was dressed so as to cause **"a man to commit adultery in his heart,"** and to be **"responsible for sending boys to hell."**

To The Unknown Daughter

I don't know whose daughter you are, but you are one of God's creatures as well as I am, hence a sister whom I love. It has been several months since I saw you there in the hospital lobby. I never met you before or since, but your face keeps coming back to me. A pleasing face, not one to win a beauty contest perhaps, but one that anyone could love. Looking at your face, I would guess you come from a good family.

My grown son was with me and we were sitting on a seat across from where you sat. I wanted to talk to you, but I am the bashful kind, not apt to start a conversation with strangers. Anyway, it's too late now, the opportunity is gone.

I can't forget the picture you made. When you walked in, your skirt was short and it wasn't tight at all. I think perhaps it might have been just as well if it had been tighter. You swung your leg up high, resting your calf on the knee of the opposite leg. It seems to me the devil himself could not devise a better way to make a man commit adultery in his heart, which is enough to keep him out of heaven.

While you sat there, I suffered intensely. I know now I should have spoken to you, even with all those people about, but I missed my chance.

Don't you have a mother? Or doesn't she care either if you are responsible for sending boys to hell where they will suffer forever (as well as yourself)? This is a strong statement but we cannot ignore the truth just because it is terrible to think about. I can't believe you didn't know how you looked. There are many others just like you in the world today and you must have seen for yourself already. Does that in any way make it better just because many others are doing it?

> There you sat for a whole hour or more in a position inexcusable for anyone except a small child. What made it all the more agonizing was the fact that you had a prayer covering on your head.
>
> Anonymous— Reprinted from *Family Life.*

———————●———————

Very little is written in the Amish literature about the dress of the male. However, many articles and letters are written about the dress of the females. This is not to say that the dress of the Amish male is unimportant; it simply is seldom written or talked about. Of course, this could be due to the fact that Amish males do practically all of the writing and it is their Biblical duty to make certain that women and children remain within the *Ordnung.*

Humility

Non-Amish writing about the Amish people almost always describe them as being a gentle, humble people. To an Amish person, humility is a virtue and pride is a cardinal sin. Often Amish homes are even without mirrors.

I have, on several occasions, been to Amish school planning meetings where humbleness (it seemed to me) almost got in the way of accomplishing that for which we were meeting. No one wants to speak first. When an Amish person speaks in their type meetings, they apologize for what they say and for speaking too long regardless of how long they spoke! An Old Order Amish writer indicates, in the following article, just how difficult it is to be genuinely humble in today's world.

———————●———————

My Struggle Against Pride

I felt pretty good about our buggy. We had given it a new coat of paint, which it had needed badly, and also made some other improvements. Being human, pride wanted to come into my heart. I wondered if other people would notice our shiny buggy, and whether they would comment on it. I tried to steer away from such thoughts, and concentrate on the real reason why we go to church. Certainly it wasn't to show off our buggy!

Satan persisted and as we were on our way to church, I was still struggling against vain thoughts. Then we passed a parked car with the words and a symbol meaning, "I love Jesus." Suddenly I felt humbled. Here I, a professing Christian, was on my way to church with my heart filled with pride, while on a "worldly" person's car was a simple meaningful expression of love to Jesus.

I cannot honestly say that Satan left me immediately, but those words gave me food for thought, and I again prayed for strength to overcome the evil within me.

Although I do not feel we should go around with bumper stickers on our buggies, I felt thankful to God that He helped me see those words at a time I needed them. Wouldn't it be good if we could carry this symbol of love to Jesus in our hearts at all time, and let it shine forth to others? Then they could see that we love Jesus.

Anonymous—Reprinted from *Family Life*

Nicknaming

Although nicknaming is common among the Amish, it is generally unknown to outsiders. The nicknames may originate from any event imaginable and will usually remain with the family down through generations. Nicknaming occurs because so many Amish have identical first and last names and this appears the only way to differentiate among themselves. Amish history indicates that there are less than fifty different last names among the over 175,000 Old Order horse and buggy Amish. Thus, nicknaming is an absolute necessity. Our family is known as "Dixie." The grapevine said this was because my grandfather purchased a farm from an outsider family named "Dixie." And David, my father's brother, was known as David "Dixie." But complications arise when brothers have sons and give them, as they frequently do, the same Biblically inspired first name. This results in one of the two (usually both) getting a first name nickname also.

An Amish person, however, never calls another Amish individual by one's nickname to one's face. It is done only in conversations with others since it is most times used only to correctly identify someone in the quickest possible manner. However, sometimes nicknames are used when making a joke or a derogatory statement about someone. And, it is personally very embarrassing for one to be called by one's nickname. However, they know that others refer to them this way. It is traditional and a way to avoid confusion in a system where so many have the same name. Females never have a first name nickname. Aside from "Dixie" there is "Bottle," "Turkey," "Tag," "Hey-Hey," "Gander," "Fish," "Cream," "Banty," "Jack," "Codger," and many, many others in my former Amish community. The father's nickname always becomes the last name of the offspring. Of course, females take on their husband's nicknames, but for the male, it is his forever. Seldom do nicknames flatter anyone. They are usually comical in nature and may be viewed by the "owner" as derogatory and even demeaning.

Church Services and Ordaining Ministers

The Old Order Amish attend church services in a member's home every other Sunday with the Sunday between set aside for visiting purposes. On this Sunday Amish people visit the homes of the sick, the homes of new babies, relatives or friends.

Depending on the size, an Amish settlement is generally divided into six church districts. That is to say, there is a North church, a Northeast church, a Northwest church and so forth. Everyone knows the particular boundaries and "orders" (rules) for each church district and will generally attend services in their own district. However, this does not mean that a member of the North district, for example, cannot attend church in the Southwest district. As stated previously, crossing church boundaries is very common, especially if the services are held in a close relative's home who lives in a neighboring district. The rules generally remain similar across the church districts within a particular community. However, there may be small, but distinct differences from one district to another. For example, in my former community, the church district permitted rubber tires on the buggy while a neighboring district had the wheels rimmed in steel. One similarity across all church districts in all Amish communities is that religious services are conducted in German.

Each church district may have as many as eight ministers and all will speak during the service which normally beings at 8:30 a.m. Usually, the minister who closes the service around one o'clock p.m. will announce in whose home services will be held two weeks from that day.

It is a large responsibility to host the church services. This means a thorough cleaning of the house and the barn, and the fences are fixed and things are painted. If it is summertime, the trees will be whitewashed (with a lime/water solution which begins to fade with the first rain) about six feet up the trunk. Of course, the woman of the house will prepare a meal to be served to everyone following the services. Cookies are served to children during the service. No longer partaking of the cookies is an obvious sign of "maturity." Older children who do take cookies are teased by their peers. This church Sunday noon meal was a tradition in my community in that it consisted only of coffee, homemade bread, jams, peanut butter thinned with maple syrup, canned beets and pickles. In my sixteen years of attending Amish church services, I observed very little variation in this particular menu. And, to my knowledge, it has not changed today.

If it is a large Amish community, three church services will be conducted in three separate homes and one will host the young people for their Sunday evening sing. That is to say, the young folks (those sixteen and older but unmarried) of the entire community gather at only one of the homes where church services were conducted that day rather than in three. The woman whose house is chosen will also prepare a meal for the young folks that evening. This meal goes far beyond the menu offered at noon. Both the church services and the evening sings spill over into the barn, especially in the large Amish districts in Lancaster, Pennsylvania.

Another duty of the host family is to go to the home where the church services were held two weeks prior and obtain the hearse-like wagon filled with the backless benches used for all religious services within the district. These backless benches are generally made of oak, are very sturdy and varnished to perfection. The family hosting church services will have pushed the furniture into corners and the benches take up the entire house. Benches will be placed upstairs, in the basement, in the main part of the house, and if need be, in the barn. The sexes remain separate during all religious services. After the members are seated (married men in the front of the preachers; young, unmarried females are seated directly behind these men; married females and small children sit in the dining room and kitchen, and others are scattered throughout the house) the *vorsinger*, the one leading the singing, begins the first song. The *vorsinger* has the informal training required but does not sit or stand in any special place. His training comes from his observation and imitation throughout the years. As stated previously, the Amish songs are not set to music, are thus difficult to sing, and to the uninformed, the singing sounds like wailing or chanting. The *vorsinger* sings the beginning of each new line of a hymn alone. The *vorsinger* duty switches to a different man with each song. The second song of every Amish church service is always the *"Lob Lied"* during which the ministers retire for council. The congregation continues to sing while the preachers are in council, but cease immediately on their return. As soon as the services end, the men carry the benches outside and the women set up the large tables for the noon meal. Men and children always eat first.

The Amish do not use trained ministers. And, as Judas' replacement was made via the casting of lots, so are Amish ministers chosen. Thus, an Amish married male may go to church on a particular Sunday as a lay person and return home that evening a minister! He will receive no compensation for this very responsible and diligent work as a minister. And, he will continue to farm and do all duties expected of any married Amish male.

No Amish person ever openly expresses a desire to be a minister as this would indicate self-pride. The only way to become a preacher is to be "hit" by the "casting of the lot." On the Sunday the new minister is to be ordained, an existing minister takes nominations from the congregation. The nominations are whispered to the ministers. As many *Ausbunds* (song books) as there are nominees are placed on a bench in front of the congregation. Only one *Ausbund* has a note saying "You are the one" (written in German) also with particular *Bible* verses, in it. Extreme anxiety surrounds the casting of the lot and sadness prevails.

Sadness is a common feeling on the day ministers are chosen. One of my uncles used to talk about this concerning himself and he was once nominated for the lot. Later he told me that he was not really concerned about getting that "particular piece of paper" (making him a minister for life) because he had not been " called" by God. I remember being present at several of these services when ministers "were made" (as the Amish call it) and on each occasion the man chosen by the lot invariably indicated that he "just knew he would get the paper." Each had felt the "call" from God to serve.

Amish ministers have no formal training and are chosen by the "casting of the lot". That is, a married Amish male may attend services on a given Sunday morning as a lay person and return home that evening as a minister for life. There is no financial compensation and ministers are expected to lead an exemplary life worthy of emulation by all. Amish sermons are long, biblically explicit and detailed. However, no notes of any sort may be used by the minister. Thus, they must spend many long hours in preparation for their Sunday delivery.

The wife of an Amish minister has no definable role to play. She simply needs to be a good housekeeper, a good wife and a good Christian. Her life is difficult for she, like her husband, is a model for other Amish to follow. Of course, it is also difficult to be an offspring of an Amish minister as the following short essay implies.

A Minister's Daughter

Even though I had a decent set of friends, I was only human and sometimes wished to make my things a little more fancy than I should have. I have never forgotten what my dear mother told me one day when I asked why I couldn't sew a wider hem on my dress. She said, "I don't believe you'd want it if you knew how many of the other girls are watching you. Seeing you with fancy things, they will say, 'She's a minister's daughter, and if she may do that, I may, too.'" My mother went on to explain that she wasn't a minister's daughter, but she watched the minister's girls and sort of used them as an example. She also told me that often our actions will affect the sermons my dad preaches. His words lost a lot of strength if his children are not abiding by the rules of the church.

This was a lesson for me. I could not help it that I was the daughter of an ordained man, but I did not want to be the reason that others went astray, or that my father's sermons would lose their effectiveness because of my disobedience. I saw that in a sense we had an added responsibility.

Anonymous—Reprinted from *Family Life*

Taking Care of Older Persons

It is nice to grow old as an Amish person. They do not use nursing homes and the elderly are revered and viewed as being wise. It is the responsibility of the young to care for the elderly—a responsibility never taken lightly.

The Amish life may seem bleak to some outsiders, but there is nothing bleak about their retirement customs. In fact, they are way ahead of modern day society when it comes to finding retirement contentment.

When an Amish farmer and his wife reach 70 or thereabouts, it is customary for them to move to a separate section of their home, or to a small house nearby known as *Grossdawdy's* (Grandfather's) *House*. Then one of their sons (usually the youngest) and his family move into the main house and take over the farming responsibilities.

The retired parents thus remain in familiar surroundings and have their privacy, yet they are close to members of their family. Although retired, there are still plenty of light chores around the farm to keep the elders happily occupied, such as tending the animals, keeping the building and grounds in order and assisting in the care of their grandchildren.

Perhaps the most appealing aspect of Amish retirement is the close relationship that is maintained with the family group. Children are taught from the cradle to "honor thy father and mother," "to take care of your own" and they generally marry and settle down within a few miles of their parents.

The close and affectionate ties which the elders thus maintain with their families, plus their firm religious faith and the economic independence, breeds an enviable contentment from most outsiders, and, in my opinion, helps avoid many of the physical and psychological ills so prevalent among the elderly of the "outsider" culture in America.

No Insurance or Involvement with the State

A large facet of Amish noninvolvement with the state is their refusal to accept government money. They turn down old-age pensions, Social Security payments and farm subsidies as unearned income and not acceptable. During World War II, a number of Amish farmers signed their milk subsidy checks over to township trustees for road maintenance. Several years ago, the state of Pennsylvania passed a law providing state aid to parochial schools and the state authorities sent a $260,000 check to the Amish school officials. The check was returned to the state unendorsed! Many, many such examples could be given.

The Amish take care of their own. Twice a year money is collected for the widows and others who are unable to earn a living. Twice yearly offerings are the only time the plate is passed in church.

Instead of buying insurance policies, the Amish have their own system of mutual aid. If a barn burns down or cattle are struck by lightning, an appraisal is made by two or three Amish males and two-thirds of the cost is paid by the church. Members are assessed according to their tax duplicates. If the amount is too large for one congregation to absorb, it is spread over several districts.

A barn raising, particularly if it is to replace a burned building, is a great social occasion. People come from miles around to help. The men raise the huge precut beams (done by Amish craftsmen who are known as excellent carpenters) into place and the women prepare food. Often times a structure is raised, roofed and covered with sideboards in a day. With hospital and medical costs rising, the Amish are facing the insurance dilemma. Some communities have gone to something known as the "Amish Aid Plan." However, the plan is controversial and is viewed as "insurance" by many Amish church groups and is thus rejected.

Holidays and Ceremonies

The Amish observe several special days as holidays. Among these are: Christmas, Good Friday, Easter, Ascension Day, Pentecost and Thanksgiving. Of course, weddings, which usually occur on Tuesday or Thursday (not during the harvest season), provide extra holidays. Barn-raisings, corn frolics and so forth also provide a type of "working" holiday for old and young alike.

Christmas was not very special at my house. And, I believe we were typical. I was never taught to believe in Santa Claus or anything even remotely similar. And, we certainly did not "cut down a young tree and foolishly bring it into the house like outsiders do" (as my father used to say) and we did not exchange presents. Each Christmas eve we children would find the largest plate available in our kitchen and set it at our individual place on the dining room table (your place at the table remains your place until you leave home) knowing that our dad would fill it with "goodies" sometime during the night. The "goodies" usually included homemade candy, nuts and caramel popcorn balls. And, on some very special times the plate may have a small package of "boughten potato chips" and "store bought candy bars."

The three holidays that I most vividly remember are Good Friday and the day preceding both the Fall and Spring Church Communion. I did not like them because they were "fasting" days, so very unusual among the Amish who are good cooks and love to eat!

The Amish and Money

I am often asked about the Amish and money. Do they use banks or other financial institutions? Are they generous with their money, etc.? In addition, non-Amish will often ask me if the Amish actually bury their money in milk cans somewhere on their property. Rumors have long persisted about this practice and they may have kept money safe in this manner years ago, especially during the depression years. However, today, most, if not all Amish, utilize banks and other financial institutions for their savings accounts, etc. However, in keeping with a Biblical dictate concerning earning interest money (usury), many Amish give any interest earned on their money to the poor, the church, etc.

Unfortunately, the Amish are perceived among their non-Amish neighbors as a parsimonious people. However, it is my opinion that they are actually generous in giving both time and money to others and are not stingy where others are concerned. However, they are a very thrifty people. The Amish always maintain extreme secrecy regarding their giving of money to others. This is in keeping with Matthew 6 where they are told to *"give, but give in secret."* Many a charity has received an envelope stuffed with cash, given by an Amish person, but without a return address or name provided.

Non-Amish individuals will sometimes inform me that they've heard that there are many wealthy people among the Amish. Again, this is basically a rumor. Although the Amish are definitely very effective at saving and handling their money, there are only a few very wealthy Amish. I do know of instances when, due to a sudden find of an abundance of under ground coal on a particular farm, an Amish farmer has suddenly come into large amounts of money. However, when this does occur, the wealth is often divided among their offspring. Of course, the church, the poor and those less fortunate, also benefit greatly from such wealth. Recently, in a *Midwestern* state, oil was discovered under several Amish farms. Although the Amish rarely sell their farms, this group quickly sold the land as farming on top of oil was too worldly for them.

Even if an Amish person is wealthy, it would be extremely sinful to appear that way. That is, if one who has lots of money and lets it be known, or behaves accordingly, would be showing taboo pride which is punishable by excommunication. Thus, regardless of the amount of money an Amish individual possesses, he or she will always appear thrifty in all they do. That is, like many non-Amish, Amish adults want it known to others about any and all good "deals" they've received; so long as this is accomplished without showing pride in their thriftiness.

The Amish are excellent traders and business people. But again, if an Amish person is wealthy, others will have difficulty observing it. For example, the church forbids buying anything for self or for others that is not **absolutely necessary**. All things considered as luxuries are forbidden by Biblical dictate: *"...abstain from luxuries, pride and carnal worldly lusts"* (1 John 2:16-17). There is a saying among the Amish: *"The bigger the manure pile the richer the owner."* This may be the only evidence of wealth one will ever see.

As the following humorous story told to me by an Amish male friend implies, there are still rumors, even among the Amish, of Amish fathers burying their money in milk cans in their back yards:

The Amish and Money: A Humorous Account

Amos Bontrager needed to go to town to the hardware store to buy a part needed to repair his walking plow so he and his wife Ruth made the trip with the horse and buggy. They had recently made a deal with a local realtor on a piece of land for $287,000. Amos tied his horse to the town's hitching post and he and Ruth walked into the realtor's office carrying two large milk cans full of cash. Amos explained to the realtor that he could count the money while he and Katie went on over to the hardware store.

"There is exactly $287,000 in these two cans," Amos said with confidence. "We'll be back soon to sign the official papers."

When he and Ruth returned to the realtor's office, the embarrassed realtor looked at Amos and said, "Amos, I'm sorry to tell you this but we counted that money in those cans five times and each time we counted we found only $284,000."

Amos, embarrassed, turned to his wife and said, "Ruth, you got the wrong cans again!"

Health and Medicine

The Amish are not opposed to physicians or scientific medicine. However, they seldom seek the advice of an MD for colds and so forth and they favor quasi-medical cures. The advice of the doctor is seldom sought until other remedies have been tried. I could document several cases of Amish people dying from what they thought was a minor ailment before seeking the advice of the "outsider" physician.

Illness becomes major news in the Amish community and is a topic of interest in the *Budget* (the Amish weekly newspaper). The length of a person's illness is often measured by how many church meetings that person misses. Sick persons are pampered by the community and friends and relatives spend much time visiting them.

Seldom do Amish women have their children delivered by an MD. This is still common today, but more and more Amish mothers are giving birth in local hospitals.

Although not opposed to surgery, dental work and anesthesia, they are often opposed to immunization. I well remember the hassle in my community when the public school authorities tried to enforce small pox immunization on the Amish. However, the authorities finally "winked" at the issue. Personally, I did not receive my Small Pox immunization until 1983 when preparing for a journey to India.

Although there are no Amish MDs, there is often an Amish person in the community who is called on to administer to the sick. This person does *Brauching*.

Sympathy-healing or *Brauching* played a role in my own Amish family. The German word *Brauch* is freely translated as "powwowing" and my grandmother was a "powwower." I was present on two occasions when she practiced her skill. Both times she moved a small shovel of red hot coals in circular motions around the "patient" and silently repeated verses and charms. Her lips moved vigorously but no words were ever uttered aloud. All the verses, charms and formulas are kept secret by the "powwower" and can only be passed along to a member of the opposite sex. Before grandmother died, in her early nineties, she passed her *Brauch* secrets along to my father (or at least I think so) who never once practiced the art. Late in his life he informed me that he simply did not believe in it. At no time was my grandmother looked upon as peculiar by other Amish people. However, we children were told not to discuss "powwowing" with "outsider" children at school as "they wouldn't understand." Such practices are still very prevalent among the Amish. However, most term the practice as "Faith Healing."

The *"brauch"* practice is currently a topic of controversy among the Amish. The following letters appearing in *Family Life* indicate that many now question the practice.

———————●———————

Faith Healing

...This practice is not dangerous because it is useless, but because it is deceptive—as the one seeking help will believe the answer is from God. People who use this practice tend to become addicted, or continually need help the same as with drugs, bringing them into bondage. Where these practices are openly accepted, many questionable things will follow, as you mention. These will not build true faith and respect in our young people....

Anonymous—Reprinted from *Family Life*

———————●———————

And, a minister writes:

———————●———————

...I'm afraid of this. Even unbelievers can do these things. By far the most conditions that people *brauch* for will correct themselves without it. Our children were able to grow up without this, even though we live next to a good neighbor who does it for various ailments. In I Timothy 4:7 Paul admonishes Timothy, "But refuse profane and old wives' fables, and exercise thyself rather unto godliness."

I believe the young folks problems can almost certainly be traced to a lack of spiritual concern on the parents' part. However, to change long-standing ungodliness, we must work together and with the church. To me that is an important part of our repentance. This cannot be brought about by placing our faith in signs and superstitions. I believe *brauching* is well meant by most who practice it, but for my part I would feel more comfortable without it.

Anonymous—Reprinted from *Family Life*

Amish people will ride a bus or hire a "driver" and travel long distances to be "cured" of an illness. News of a "good doctor who can really cure" travels fast in an Amish community and this particular physician suddenly finds himself (they would not seek out a female physician) with several new Amish patients. Also, "doctor changing," much to the dislike of outsider physicians, is common among the Amish people.

Sadly, many Amish people are taken in by quacks. The *Budget* carries advertisements for all sorts of ointments and other type medicines that the Amish regularly purchase (see *The Amish Newspaper—the Budget*, page 111).

Traveling to Mexico for Medical Assistance

The Old Order Amish may have been the first Americans to endorse and seek medical treatment in a foreign country. Hundreds of Old Order Amish from across the US travel to Mexico for medical treatment, especially for expensive surgeries. Tijuana is the city of choice and they report that the medical facilities there are clean and that they almost always receive their test results in one day. In addition, and most important to the Amish, they report that the

Mexican medical staffs are courteous, accepting and understanding of their way of life. The Amish who have traveled to Mexico for treatment also report that they find the prices very reasonable and manageable and much lower than here in the US. And, since they do not carry health insurance the Amish see this as a "Heaven-sent" blessing. The numbers of Amish making this excursion are expected to increase dramatically as medical costs continue to rise in the US. Many ride a train down while others hire an "English" driver to take them to Mexico. They believe strongly that, even with the cost of the trip to Mexico, they still save large sums of money in the long run and that they will always receive excellent medical care there.

Hundreds of Amish Participating in Modern Medical Research

The Amish, who typical shun technology, are assisting two Harvard educated scientists in unlocking the mysteries of human genetic makeup as well as willingly participating in other important medical research projects **(USA Today, June 27, 2005).** The Amish research facility was built by the Amish and is located in the middle of a field in central Pennsylvania. Housed in the facility is a **Clinic for Special Children** along with the **Amish Research Clinic. The Clinic for Special Children** is viewed by the Amish as a true blessing from God and Amish parents from across the country bring their "special" children to the clinic for treatment. Amish children are disproportionally afflicted by often fatal, genetically based diseases the direct result of the centuries of intermarriage within the sect. Sadly, the numbers of such special Amish children, always cared for at home by family and relatives, are growing in leaps and bounds. There are eighty such children in my former Amish community alone, a small Amish community by comparison. I am personally acquainted with an Amish couple with nine (9) children, five (5) of whom are in wheelchairs as the result of the same genetically based disease. Many an Amish child's life has been saved by the medical staff at this **Clinic for Special Children** in the Amish heart land in rural Pennsylvania..

The **Amish Research Clinic** has played a major role in many significant discoveries from diabetes to helping solve the mystery of infant death syndrome. With the help of a ten million dollar grant from the National Institutes of Health, the researchers are also conducting heart and longevity studies among the Amish.

The Amish, like the Ashke Jews and some Indian tribes with insular, homogenous gene pools, offer the researchers unparalleled opportunities to gain insight into diseases and genetics. As of this writing, more than 3000 Amish have had their blood drawn by the research scientists. The Amish view their participation with the "English" scientists as just one more way of "helping their fellow man" as dictated by their religious beliefs. Much of the on going financing for the two scientists is raised by community auctions that sell quilts, hand crafted grandfather clocks, home made furniture, baked goods, etc. donated by the Old Order Amish.

Homemade Medical Remedies

The Amish have always been extremely fond of homemade medical remedies and the Amish newspaper, The Budget, prints several requests from readers for "cures" for certain ailments or afflictions on a weekly basis. Hundreds of such Amish remedies could be printed here but I will give just one; the one for an ailment for which all of us would appreciate a "cure."

For Colds

Boil one gallon dandelion flowers and one gallon hot water for five minutes. Let stand for three days. (It is best kept in a crock jug.) Strain. Then boil the peelings of two lemons and one orange with the dandelion water for 15 minutes. Let stand until luke-warm. Slice in the two lemons and the orange. Add two teaspoons yeast and three pounds of sugar and let stand for six days. Bottle.

Anonymous—from *Family Life*

Practicing the Common Courtesies

As mentioned previously, the Amish parents do not always teach their children that which the outsider terms "common courtesies." *Family Life* carried several essays, both pro and con, concerning the notion of knocking on a neighbor's door before entering. The following essay best explains their reasons for not knocking.

Door Knocking

...It is a challenge for each of us to try to regulate the affairs of our household so that if anyone were to step inside the front door unannounced we would not need to be ashamed. It is an unwritten law that among our people we do not take baths, or appear half-dressed, inside the front door. We have private rooms where we go to take care of our private needs and it is well that it is so. I would like to relate an incident which happened a number of years ago to illustrate this point.

Early one morning a man went to his neighbor's house to make arrangements for the day's work. As he stepped inside the door, the family, and it was a large family, was at the breakfast table. His entrance took them a bit by surprise, and before he had time to see what was going on, one of the girls quickly rose from the table and made a hasty departure to the upstairs of the house. The truth was that she was not dressed as was fitting for anyone to be at the breakfast table. That was the reason for her sudden departure.

Who was at fault? Was it the unexpected visitor, or was it the girl who insisted on coming to the breakfast table in such a state as not to be presentable to the neighbor? I am afraid it was the latter, and if we are to maintain the simplicity of our way of life, then we will have to keep up our standards that we are ready to welcome our brother at any time of the day at least inside of the front door.

Most of our houses are built so we can see the lane from the kitchen table. Where this is not the case, then it would be especially wise to announce our coming in some way such as slamming a door in going through the summer kitchen or in some other way. If we open the main door slowly, it immediately signifies that someone else except a member of the family is there (Who ever heard of a member of the family opening the door slowly?) Once inside the door, if no one is present, we can listen if perhaps the family is engaged in family devotions or other matters which would be private. If this is not the case then we can always say "Hello" or some other word of greeting which will announce our presence in a way that should not be embarrassing.

Looking in the *Bible*, we cannot find anything definite on the matter.

When Peter escaped from prison he knocked at the door where the church was assembled (Acts. 12:13). But this really does not prove anything because due to obvious reasons the door was locked and this was the only way in which he could make his presence known. We would hardly believe, that he would have taken the time to knock if the door would have been unbarred.

Anonymous—Reprinted from *Family Life*

The Amish Newspaper—the *Budget*

Most Amish do not subscribe to *"worldly"* daily newspapers or other similar publications, as the *Budget* is the weekly newspaper for the Amish people. Scribes, one or two from each Amish community, write the news of their particular community to the *Budget* offices in Sugarcreek, Ohio on a weekly basis. The letters are edited and printed in a plain looking newspaper which is sent out to thousands of Amish subscribers.

The *Budget* has been in existence for more than a hundred years and serves as a pipeline of communication between Amish and Mennonite communities around the world. Although there are, in general, 4 or 5 pages of advertisements, the structure of the *Budget* is simply a set of single 3 inch wide columns written weekly by some 400 "Scribes" from some 30 States, Canada and 5 or so foreign countries. For example, an August, 2004 edition included pieces written by scribes from 36 different states and 7 foreign countries. In this particular edition, the state represented by the most writers was Ohio with scribes representing 107 Amish settlements. Pennsylvania was next with 33 while Indiana had columns written by 31 scribes.

The paper is unique in many respects. It has no staff writers, editorials, crossword puzzles or comic strips. Its strength, style and tone are derived from the "letters" from the unpaid correspondents.

The heading of each column gives the name of the Amish scribe's home community and concludes with his/her name. Some of the columns are quite lengthy but most are 500 -700 words or so in length. There are no headlines, no photographs and nothing is ever written in the *Budget* concerning politics and very, very little about crime.

The scribes' only remuneration is a complimentary subscription to the paper, some writing paper, and mailing envelopes provided by the *Budget* home office. The editor, an outsider, has the task of sifting through approximately 400 scribes' weekly, handwritten dispatches. Letters from towns like Charm, Intercourse, Viroqua, Horse Cave, Gallipolis, Mesopotamia and Punxsutawney have to be edited for grammar and punctuation. This is a difficult task since the scribes' second language is English and most speak fluent Pennsylvania Dutch. For the Amish scribes, writing in perfect English is difficult, at least for most. Fractured syntax is often in evidence in the columns.

Only one small corner of one page (two columns) of the *Budget* is written in German, or Pennsylvania Dutch. The column is titled: *Es Pennsilfaanisch Deitsch Eck* (The Pennsylvania Dutch Corner) and is usually reserved for poetry, short essays on history, etc. Another page has a regular section titled; *Obituaries and in Memoriams.*

The scribes report with simplicity that, **"Somebody innocently walked off with the wrong hat at _____ 's funeral."** and, **"_____'s driving horse took real sick and was in a bad way for several days."** Another wrote (March 7, 2001), **_____ 's shawl was missing after church last Sunday and this is the only one she has so please check your shawls.** A scribe wrote recently that **"_____ is losing out and it don't look too good for her."**

Weather is very important to the Amish. It dictates their daily lives and is paramount to their livelihood. It is a major topic each week in the *Budget* and some 95% of the columns begin with a report of the weather for that particular day or week as it concerns the writer's area of the country. For example, The column from Gladwin, Michigan (October 25, 2000) begins: **"Nice Fall weather last week. Corn looks like it's ready to husk."** And from Mount Gilead, Ohio

(*Budget*, November 8, 2000), **"This is a nice frosty sunny fall morning, which we had the same most of last week. Had a wee bit of rain early Friday morning, then cooled off again."** On November 15, 2000, a scribe from an Amish community in Ohio wrote: **"The weather is turning more damp and colder. Just right for the wedding season to start."** Another from Pennsylvania writes; **"Reports are at Eric they got 2 feet of that white stuff awhile ago! If I hear the hoot owl at night it means its getting warmer."** A March 2001 column began with, **"The birds are beginning to sing and spring is on the way. It is time to start the spring farm work."**

News of the weather, announcing a "frolic" *(when the Amish men gather to help an ailing neighbor build a new barn or when the women gather to assist a new mother with the canning of fruits and vegetables, etc.)*, the crops, births, health, weddings, funerals, and the location of the next week's church services are a part of most every column. In addition, the scribes almost always provide the names of Amish from other communities who were recent visitors to his/her community, the names of those individuals who missed last Sunday's service because of illness, etc. Such news items appear in the folksy *Budget* on a weekly basis.

On occasion, amazing (and often amusing) stories appear in a scribe's column. For example, in a column from the November 8, 2000 edition, the scribe from _____, Pennsylvania writes: **"Is anyone interested in a new method to catch mice? Recently, aunt _____ was at her sewing machine and had just begun sewing when she was startled by a frantic squeaking. She found a mouse hanging from the sewing machine belt. It was caught by the tail and was trying to kick itself loose!"** And from _____, Indiana (October 18, 2000): **"We hope _____ doesn't get tired pedaling her sewing machine in the next few weeks. _____ was on a trip and put her dirty clothes in a bag and left the bag in the washhouse. Later the boys were told to burn the trash and they grabbed all the bags that were there to later discover that one of those bags was _____'s clothes!"** In a March, 2001 edition of the *Budget*, a scribe writes about a non-Amish neighbor whose mother had mailed her a gift of homemade cookies, along with some special biscuits for her pet dog. Evidently the lady did not know they were dog biscuits and ended up eating several after dunking them in coffee. The Amish scribe writes: **"Well, they did seem a little hard but she felt maybe they were just getting old and when soaked in coffee they were quite tasty and she ate quite** a few. Later when her kids got home from school she told them about the hard cookies and they checked them out and insisted that they were doggie cookies. _____ didn't want to believe it but a phone call to her mother confirmed the truth!"

As noted, the Amish are a very kind, generous and helpful people. This is best depicted in a section of each weekly *Budget* labeled *"Showers." "Showers"* are announcements requesting that cards be sent to an ailing person who **"needs cheering up"** or that money be sent to someone who can no longer work because of injury or sickness, etc. It should be acknowledged that in the absence of insurance and social security benefits, many Amish families rely on this type of assistance for their medical emergencies. For example, in the January 24, 2001 edition, a *Budget* subscriber wrote; **"Let's have a money shower for _____. He has no income and needs lots of medicine."** In the January 10, 2001 *Budget,* a subscriber wrote, in part: **"Let's have a shower of money and letters of encouragement for _____, age 42. He had numerous seizures of an enlarged blood vessel in his head which caused unconsciousness."** And another request, one of 30 shower announcements appearing in the same edition, states: **"Let's have a get well letter or whatever you want wish shower for _____. He has a badly broken wrist after falling off a barn roof."** And appearing in the December 20, 2000 *Budget*: **"Let's have a get well and money shower for _____. He had an accident while shoeing horses smashing a finger. He is a bleeder."** In the March 7, 2001 edition of the *Budget,* a reader wrote; **"Let's help a couple who opened their hearts and gave two little orphans from Romania a home. Adoption expenses were around $19,000."** Of course, the writer's name is always given along with the specific address of the proposed shower recipient. There is also a section titled simply, *"Cards of Thanks."* These are short, reprinted thank you notes from the recipients of the above described shower requests.

In the absence of a daily newspaper, *Budget* scribes often summarize a bit of news that they've heard from a worldly neighbor, the outsider milkman, the mailman or whomever. For example, recently a *Budget* scribe wrote about a meteor shower that someone had told him about: ."**...a fist-sized meteor hit their parked car at night. The occupants of the house heard a boom and felt the shock through the ground."** The same scribe also wrote: **"In the year 1900 an official survey estimated that there were less than 500,000** white-tailed deer in the United States. Today there are nearly 19 million of these fine animals in the nation." One scribe provided a vivid detail of a robbery that occurred at a fruit market in her community during the first week of the New Year (January 3, 2001). Another one wrote (December 27, 2000), **A good cow took sick and was off feed for _____ Yoder with the vet diagnosing it as twisted intestines."** Such tidbits of news are commonplace in the *Budget.*

Each edition of the *Budget* also contains two or three pages of advertisements aimed specifically at the Amish buyer. Recent ads (2004) included a drawing of a modern looking blender with a handle attached so that one can operate it in the absence of electricity, non-electric stove top waffle iron, nylon draft buggy horse harnesses, horse shoes, walking plows, all types of cheese, oil lamps for the home and barn, animal remedies from nature, dry goods, water pumping windmills, horse neck yokes, steel wheels, leather working tools, 60 inch diameter black buggy umbrellas and a rather large ad touting "Go Greyhound."

Non-Amish will sometimes place *Budget* ads for Amish carpenters, brick layers, domestics, etc. in the *Budget*. A relatively recent phenomenon is seeing "outsider" adoption agencies occasionally advertised in the *Budget*. Also, non-Amish children and youth often advertise in the *Budget* requesting Amish pen pals. A recent such classified advertisement stated: *"Pen Pals, all ages for 'English' youth, male and female, very interested in Amish faith and life. Please write soon to..."*

As discussed in a previous section, there have long been Old Order Amish faith healers and the Amish have a reputation (some rumored, some factual) for trying almost anything to help them with a persistent medical problem. Unfortunately, they are often taken advantage of by unscrupulous individuals hoping to make a quick profit. Practically every edition of the *Budget* contains advertisements for herbs and other remedies, that in my opinion are not only untested and unscientific, but possibly harmful. For example, recently, an edition of the *Budget* contained a large advertisement that began: *"If you are over 35 you need to clear out your arteries!"* The ad was for a type of *"heart drop"* that would, according to the vendor, *"Prevent heart attacks, strokes, aneurysms, prevent clogging of arteries, shrink swollen enlarged hearts,"* among other claims. Another one appearing in a later edition advertised an *artery cleaner capsule* to be taken with each meal. The claim was that this pill also,

---

"...strengthens the heart muscles and purifies the blood." Another ad was for a *"...natural... safe way to eliminate Candida... people no longer have to live with fatigue, gas, poor elimination, poor digestion, sugar cravings, moodiness, brain fog, cold hands and feet, digestive bloat... etc.*

The *Budget* also contains many advertisements for various natural supplements and herbs with various, and often dubious medical claims. The Amish have also been known to travel long distances, even to foreign countries, seeking a "cure" and some of these medical clinics aggressively seek Amish patients. For example, the August, 2004 edition of the *Budget* carried a two column-wide advertisement for a medical clinic in Tijuana, Mexico. The latter advertisement gave the specific dates and times when and where the director of this Mexican clinic would be appearing for "get acquainted" meetings with interested Amish people. The meetings were scheduled in several different US Amish communities.

The fact that the Amish have a strong desire for assistance of any kind with their medical problems can also be observed in a weekly *Budget* section called, *"Information Please."* For example, in a January 2001 edition *"Information Please"* section, a reader writes, **"Is there anything that can be done for sleeping hands....?"** Another reader writes, **"Does any reader have multiple sclerosis? I have a daughter-in-law that has this. What did you find that would help?"** Another writes, **"If you have a good answer for migraine headaches, please write to...."** A *Budget* reader writes (January 10, 2001), **"Is there someone in *Budget* land that would know of an herb or diet that would dissolve or help fibrosystic disease or fibrostic cysts."** Writers' names and addresses are given and then answers or suggestions that others wish to share appear in a later issue.

In a recent edition of the *Budget's "Information Please"* section, a reader gave an answer to someone who had asked about how to cure "heart flutter; **"In answer to the heart flutter problem, consider the cause! Working too hard, also overeating. Taking a tablespoon of flax seed each day prevents heart attack...."** Another writes; **"Varicose veins and leg sores are usually caused by eating too many different things together and causes digestive problems. Eat one food each meal if problem with digestion."** Often there are also inquires about remedies for sick animals appearing in this section of the *Budget*.

However, it is my opinion that most Amish people seek the appropriate medical attention and advice for their ailments.

The *"Information Please "* section of the *Budget* is not limited to medical questions and answers. Questions such as **"What can I do for blight on black raspberries? How do I keep the birds away from them?"** or, **"Does anyone in *Budget* land know where I can buy a one quart butter churn?"** Amish readers are rather concrete in their answers to someone who has asked a question in this section: **"Tie aluminum pie pans to the branches of blueberry bushes. The noise when the wind blows them together and the shiny appearance will keep birds out of the berries."**

Of course, the important Amish news that has occurred in the specific scribe's community during the previous week is given. Some examples *(the first names have been changed and the last names omitted):*

News from a scribe in Pennsylvania was that, **"Amos ____ missed church again Sunday because of being kicked out cold by a horse."** Elsewhere in her column, the scribe from a Midwestern Amish community reported without comment that **"John ____ spend Sunday at _____ to remind him of his 40th birthday."** And from an Amish settlement in Indiana came word that a **"Little dishwasher came to stay at Amos ____'s since 18th Dec..., named Rebecca. She is welcomed by 8 brothers and 2 sisters."**

The contributors to the *Budget* often end their specific letter (column) with a famous quote or something witty they themselves have written or heard from others. For example, one such recent quote was: **"People who are always making allowances for themselves soon go bankrupt."** Another ended her column with; **"A knowledge of the *Bible* is better than a college course."** Still another wrote; **"Lighthouses don't ring bells to call attention to their light, they just shine."**

To the average reader of today's newspapers, some of the above items might seem trivial and even quaint. However, for the Amish people, this news is of utmost importance. For them, the world is chronicled in seven gray columns covering 30 to 35 pages of the weekly *Budget* and they eagerly anticipate its delivery to their rural mailboxes.

Additional Avenues of Communication

For many Amish the *Budget* is the only newspaper to enter their home. However, many now subscribe to the three Amish magazines published by Amish people in Alymer, Ontario. The three are: *Family Life, Blackboard Bulletin* and *Young Life.*

Family Life contains Views and Values, letters to the editor, World Wide Window, Staff Notes, Learning About Your Health, a Children's Section and stories relating to the Amish heritage, among many others. Its founding date was 1967.

The Blackboard Bulletin replaced the "circle letter" among Amish school teachers. A monthly publication, it focuses mainly on problems relating to Amish education. Each issue contains several teaching tips, written by Amish teachers, along with several essays written by Amish school children.

Young Life is written for young Amish adults and focuses on courtship practices and other aspects relating to Amish youth. Much is currently being written concerning the problem Amish youth are having in maintaining their values and customs.

Many more Amish rules for living could be written. However, the basic rules and regulations governing the lives of the Amish have been covered in this section.

Section V

Courtship, Marriage and Death

Amish courting begins at age sixteen in most Amish communities and is known as *rum springa* or "running around." This age limit is strictly enforced by the other unmarried young people who are sixteen and beyond. Should a young man (in my former community) attend one of the Sunday evening Amish sings before his sixteenth birthday, he is teased and forcibly fed warm milk from a spoon. This playful ritual indicates to the young man that he is not yet mature enough to attend the "sings" and to date. Females not yet sixteen simply do not attend the Sunday evening sings (called "crowds"). This would reveal a rebellious nature that would not be tolerated.

Most everyone knows the exact day of a youth's sixteenth birthday and young men often look forward to a particular pretty young maiden's sixteenth birthday—it is a rite of passage! It is obvious that young Amish males and females yearn for their sixteenth birthday. In my former Amish community, age sixteen is viewed as a time of reaching adulthood—legislated maturity by the community. Upon reaching your sixteenth birthday, the Sunday afternoon becomes yours and you no longer are obligated to go home with your parents following church services to do the Sunday evening chores. To be given a Sunday evening free of farm-related chores is envied by one's younger siblings. In addition, a male is usually presented a horse and buggy as his own for his sixteenth birthday. In some communities, women are required to wear a loose fitting cape-like apron over their dress in keeping with their concept of modesty.

As mentioned in a previous section, church services are held in several homes simultaneously if the size of the Amish community so warrants. However, the youth singing, or "crowd" as termed in most communities, will generally be held in only *one* home that Sunday evening. The location of the singing is often a mystery. Yet, somehow, the youth from all the different church districts within that respective community seem to learn the location of the "crowd" and shortly after the "old-folks" leave the church services, the young folks begin to appear from throughout the community. A large meal is served to all by the host and hostess. The custom of keeping the sexes segregated during the church services also applies at the Sunday evening singing. For several hours or so the youth will sing and hold conversations. Of course, as in any group, not all the Amish youth will be inside the house singing. The Amish have their share of both males and females who break the rules and are sometimes seen as trouble-makers by the adults. Some of these "trouble-makers" may even bring home-brew to the "crowd," or may even have purchased beer or whiskey for the occasion. The only married people at the singing will be the owners of the particular farm where the youth are gathered. However, if the father of the household permits this forbidden type of activity to occur, he faces the wrath of the ministers and parents. Thus, many an Amish farmer has attempted to run the young, deviant trouble-makers from his farm. As can be imagined, most of the youth cannot get into the house and much of the singing and games occur in the barn and other locations. In the absence of modern lighting, exactly what goes on outside the house is sometimes difficult to control.

It is a well-known fact that Amish parents are lenient (it is almost a casual look-the-other-way attitude by some) with their sons who are between the age of sixteen and marriage. And, some young men (those who stay outside rather than go into the house to sing, for example) go on a "binge" or go "wild." It should be acknowledged that the term "wild" has different connotations for different cultures, i.e. (as stated in the following essay) making wise cracks and telling jokes are signs of being "wild" to the Amish adults. However, Amish adults nag these types of boys to "settle down." Two Amish adults write about this **"wild"** stage in the following letters to *Family Life*.

———————●———————

Our Children Need Their Parents

Something is wrong in our Christian churches but where is the root of the trouble? Children are running after the pleasures of this world. They smoke, drink, make wisecracks, run with the *wild* bunch, have smaller and smaller coverings and shorter dresses. They hide things they're not supposed to have so the parents don't find out. Why are they different from what Christian young folks used to be? Are they afraid of being looked down upon? Why do they come home and bring us the faults of others to try to cover up their own? Why do we as parents repeat these things to others behind their backs? Is it because of a lack of true Christian principles?

Have we taught our children to love their neighbors and not gossip about them or relate their faults to others? Or do we as parents still do these things? If we do, there is no wonder our children are doing them.

Anonymous—Reprinted from *Family Life*

———————●———————

Settling Down

It's a dangerous thing to pressure someone into "settling down" without insisting that he also "settle up." For it is quite possible for a young person to decide, when he gets tired of being nagged by the church and parents, that okay, he'll conform. He may be ready to get married anyhow, and stay at home. So he agrees to drop his "wild life," whatever that may include in his particular community. And relatives and parents, looking only on the outside, draw a sigh of relief—too soon. Far too often such a person has not really experienced an inner change. He has not really given himself up, surrendered and dedicated his life to God. What he does is not out of conviction. There is not depth to his spiritual life. He does not think to go aside for personal prayer. He does not cherish a tender conscience and a daily walk with God. The Bible doesn't interest him.

Thus the sowing-wild-oats-and-settling-down-later pattern becomes expected of young people—it is almost a family tradition, and the parents may become alarmed if their children don't follow it than if they do. But, no matter how accepted such reasoning and behavior has become in some communities, it is unscriptural. It is a blight on the church. It is unfair to young people, who often find out to their sorrow that they must reap what they have sown. We need to awaken to the spiritual harm this type of reasoning has done, and will continue to do unless it is stopped.

Reprinted from *Family Life*

⸻ ● ⸻

The formal singing at the "crowd" generally concludes around 10:00 p.m. However, in most communities the young people do not pair off and go home at this hour. Rather, they play "ring" type games. These games are tolerated, but most adults (even though they may have taken part in them when young) question whether or not they are Christian activities.

The games are often played late into the night, however, couples usually begin to pair off around midnight. A young Amish man does not directly ask a girl for a date. He sends a "middle-man" to ask a particular girl to be his date following the "crowd." Even couples who are going steady will usually meet at a pre-arranged time or the young man will send a buddy to let his girlfriend know that he is now ready to take her home. Usually, especially if it is a first date, the young man will attempt to slip away from the singing without being noticed. If it is the first date, he will most certainly be followed to the young lady's home by a group of his Amish male and female friends. In my community, people who follow the young couple home are known as "cut-ups." They harass the young couple. They may remove the wheels from his buggy, turn his horse loose or do other types of mischievous deeds while he is attempting to court the young lady. The young lady's parents remain in the house and try to appear unconcerned. I remember one particular incident in which the "cut-ups" worked very hard taking a young man's buggy apart and rebuilt it straddle of the barn's roof peak—40 feet up!

Young men and women who have an interest in each other for dating purposes will seldom be seen together in daylight. Thus, a brother may bring his sister or a female cousin to the Sunday evening singing. These young people can be observed in any Amish community on a Sunday afternoon as they travel toward the singing in their open buggies. Should the buggy be overcrowded, the young men will be seated on the laps of the females. The reverse will not be observed. This is in keeping with the dominance of the male.

It is a commonly known fact that young Amish men spend a considerable amount of time at their date's home. Many a young Amish man has been seen traveling home in his buggy on a Monday morning as the sun is rising—sound asleep! However, when he does arrive home, he will receive no pity from his parents and will work the entire day. He will not get an opportunity to sleep until after the evening meal.

This practice of staying at his date's house until the wee hours of the morning may be the remnants of the courtship practice of bundling, which used to be prevalent in many Amish communities. There may still be Amish communities that practice bundling, or as it is often termed, "bed-courtship."

The practice of bundling has been defended by some Amish people on the basis that it was tradition, and tradition is sacred among the Amish. However, most Amish now condemn this practice. A recently married Amish female wrote the following letter to *Family Life* concerning her past bundling.

No More Bundling

I am thankful for the discipline my parents taught me, although at the time it all seemed so harsh, but now I feel it was not harsh enough. Since I'm married I've told them how glad I am that they made me dress plainly at all times and didn't allow me to go swimming, even though I cried then because I couldn't go. Now I have a sister who has just turned sixteen and already is going steady with a boy (whom I hold nothing against) but feel she is too young yet.

I told her if I could live that time of my life over again I wouldn't start dating until I'm at least eighteen. Nor would I practice bundling or go away that would require a stay overnight. Nor would I consider visiting with each other later than midnight necessary. All the talking, singing or reading can be done before this hour; longer visits only lead to other things which are not good.

Anonymous—Reprinted from *Family Life*

It is the writer's belief, based on the writing of Amish adults, that bundling will shortly be, if not already, a thing of the past for the Amish. It should be acknowledged that most Amish adults do not permit their children to bundle.

Because of uninformed non-Amish writers, many are led to believe that the Amish practice immoral courtship. However, this is simply not true. A letter was sent to *Young Companion* by a young Amish person seeking advice about what to do on a date. Some of the answers the person received in the next issue indicate that *most* Amish communities not only do not permit bed courtship but even discourage hand holding and especially "**kissing and hugging**."

---•---

Courtship

I may be wrong, but I am convinced most sincere young people conduct their courtship exactly in the way that is expected of them. The trouble is that their parents and the church do not expect enough. Nearly twenty years ago my wife and I were the first dating couple in a new Amish settlement where, I am thankful to say, high Christian standards were expected of us.

The church asked us to not see each other more often than once a week (less frequently at first); to be with each other no more than a few hours at a time; to always visit with each other in a well-lighted room. Hugging, kissing or petting were strictly out....

Anonymous—Reprinted from *Young Companion*

---•---

Premarital sex relations are disapproved of and condemned by the Amish elders and community. Transgressors are expelled from the church and shunned. However, reinstatement requires only a confession before the church assembly and a moral stigma does not remain with the couple.

There is a very low rate of illegitimate births among the Amish. It is common knowledge that in the case of an illegitimate pregnancy, marriage will follow. Rarely, if ever, is a great deal of pressure on the couple necessary. In rare cases when the identification of the father is questionable, an older man in the community, usually a widower, will marry the mother-to-be and raise the child as his own. If the child is born out of wedlock it is usually taken into the family by the girl's parents and, since marriage almost always follows shortly thereafter, the social or moral stigma is not lasting.

An Amish mother apologizes for the **"way we got married"** in the following letter to *Young Companion*.

...Yes, there a quite a few things I would do different if I could do them over again. The first thing is I would listen more to what my mother and father say. I would join church, not only because I had the age and everyone else did, but because I wanted to be born again. I'd want my husband and I to have a different courtship. How much better it would have been if we would not have kept such late hours. Maybe then we wouldn't have had a baby six months after we were married. We asked forgiveness before God and church, but we still have to reap what we sowed. We have to try and explain to our children to do as we say, not as we did.... I'm not sorry that I married who I did, and hope he feels the same way, too. But I'm sorry for the way we got married. So all you boys and girls, remember, what you sow that you must someday reap.

Anonymous—Reprinted from *Young Companion*

Because of the limited number of available marriage partners, there has always been a great deal of inbreeding among the Amish. Deleterious effects, such as a sixth finger or underdeveloped third breast in females are sometimes a direct result of inbreeding. Marriage between first cousins is now taboo and second cousin marriages, though frequent, are officially discouraged by the church. (This is discussed in more detail in Section VII.) However, to say the least, mate finding is sometimes difficult in a small Amish community where marrying "outside the faith" is strictly forbidden.

An Amish youth is permitted to marry a member of a more conservative church, but to marry someone from a more liberal Amish church group is forbidden. Because of scarcity of marriageable mates, it is becoming a common practice for a group of dating-age young people to spend a weekend visiting another Amish community. These groups visit one another usually via Greyhound buses and are known in the community as "strangers." The young people look forward to this group of "strangers." It is always a much talked-about occasion when word is received that a group of "strangers" from a distant Amish community will be visiting for the weekend.

There are basically only 50 or so different last names among the Amish. Thus, it is not at all uncommon for a young lady not to change her last name when she marries, i.e., Wittmers frequently marry Wittmers, Yoders marry Yoders and Bontragers marry Bontragers.

As mentioned previously, dating begins at age sixteen. However, the magic surrounding age sixteen is being questioned by both some young and older Amish. This questioning is evident in the following letters.

―――――――●――――――――

Dating Age

I think there is danger in dating too young, especially at sixteen. I myself started at seventeen and see now that it was bad because I was not serious about it and so dated many girls just for a good time. You might be serious at sixteen even if I wasn't, but I would still recommend waiting for a few years. By that time you would be able to consider marriage after dating for a suitable period.

Anonymous—Reprinted from *Young Companion*

―――――――●――――――――

I think parents should discourage sixteen and 17'ers from dating and going steady, instead of being proud of them when they do. Maybe if they would know everything, their proudness would turn to shame. Unless most sixteen and 17'ers are more mature than I was at that age it is best not to get serious about this, which is something that should not be anything but serious.

Anonymous—Reprinted from *Young Companion*

―――――――●――――――――

Some Amish communities have strict rules for determining the "dating age." However, it is my opinion that age sixteen is the norm. But, as indicated in a letter to *Young Companion,* some communities discourage dating at sixteen.

———————●◄———————

...In our area the "hands off" way of courtship is upheld, and we also discourage dating before the age of 18. Many of them do wait until they are 18 or older, for which we are grateful.

Anonymous—Reprinted from *Young Companion*

———————●◄———————

The term "dating" was not used in my former community except in jest. They may use the word "dating" or "date" to mock, or make fun of, a custom held by the outsiders. However, within my community it is customary to use the word "have" rather than "date." That is to say, the young person will be asked, "Whom did you *have* last Sunday?" However, "having" as used in this context does not have any sexual connotations.

Once a young man and woman are going steady, he not only will date her on Sunday evenings but may also appear at her house during the week. On this week night the young man will not make his appearance known until the rest of her family is in bed. That is to say, even if he has to wait at the end of the lane in the cold, he does not appear until all the lights in the house have gone out. However, she will know that he is coming and will be awaiting his arrival. He may toss a small pebble or a kernel of corn against her window to let her know of his arrival but usually the dog's bark will be enough to alert her. Standard equipment for a young man of this age includes a flashlight. By the use of a flashlight, he can also let his female friend know of his arrival.

Usually the young man comes into the house and stays until the wee hours of the morning. If they are serious about one another, they will discuss the upcoming wedding. She will tell him about her dowry which had been started very early in her life and continues until she marries. The dowry usually contains homemade quilts, gifts, silverware and other types of useful things. As previously mentioned, Amish couples work diligently to maintain the secrecy and are seldom, if ever, seen together in daylight before the "banns are published" for their marriage.

As previously mentioned, premarital intercourse is not condoned and should an unmarried couple have engaged in such activity, they will both make a public confession and will be shunned for a period of at least two weeks. As stated before, no stigma is attached to this type of activity and it is not considered among the "worst sins." Also, should she be pregnant the number of months following their marriage and the birth of the child is not really that important. Outside observers (who know of such occurrences) find it difficult to believe the lack of a stigma in such cases.

There is mounting evidence that Old Order Amish females of marrying age far outnumber the men. An Amish writer in an issue of *Young Companion* asked why and suggested an answer.

---•---

Why So Many Single Girls?

I am surprised that nearly everyone seems to think single girls should readily accept it as God's will that they remain single. There is very little difference in the birth rate between male and female, which shows me that in general it is God's will for each one to have a life companion to love and to respect. What is the reason there are so many single girls left? Is it not because so many of our boys leave our faith in their young days? Now, do you think that is God's will? Are we teaching them the way they should go?

Anonymous—Reprinted from *Young Companion*

---•---

Marriage

The entire courtship process is conducted with secrecy, and ideally, it is an admirable feat to keep the seriousness of the relationship a secret until the reading of the banns which are published two weeks prior to the wedding.

The rationale behind the secrecy in courtship seems to not have a definite explanation, but appears to be a traditional pattern. It may be conjectured that such secrecy is in line with avoidance of using married couples given names in public and disapproval of public displays of affection.

Of course, the neighborhood realizes when a couple has been going "steady" for quite some time that the wedding is approaching. Thus, since there is nothing equal to an engagement the neighbors often look for telltale signs of the approaching marriage. Marriages are generally held on Tuesdays and Thursdays during the months of November and December. These months follow the busy time of the harvest. A good sign of an approaching wedding is when her family plants a larger than usual garden in the Spring.

When a young couple decides they are ready for marriage, the young man follows a secret, strict, formal plan. He will send a middle man again, as he did while dating, to the bride-to-be parents, who subsequently asks for her hand in marriage. Her parents will already have been alerted and the middle man is simply a traditional formality. However, the middle man always makes his approach in extreme secrecy and will travel to the bride-to-be's home after dark. Once the girl's parents have consented to the marriage, the ministers are involved. They travel to the homes of both youths and counsel with them. Their traveling is also done in secrecy usually following darkness.

If either the middle man or the ministers are seen traveling to the respective homes, the rumors spread quickly. If the two sets of parents, the ministers, the middle man and the two people to be married can maintain this secret until the banns are publicly published, the couple has "pulled one off on the community." Should the plans be found out before the banns are published, the young couple will be visited and noisy shiverreeing of both of their homes takes place. The young man is considered somewhat of a hero if he can maintain this secrecy. The fact that people in the community did not learn of the wedding plans is talked about for many months and maybe even years.

Following the announcement of the upcoming marriage, the couple begins the big plans. The "published" bridegroom may move in with her parents until the wedding. He is highly involved in getting the house cleaned up, especially on the outside, and also in readying the barn for games and so forth. Also, he will help to whitewash the trees and will paint different buildings. As previously mentioned, whitewashing with a mixture of lime and water is a common beautifying activity among the Amish. The trees will be whitewashed from the ground up to about six feet. Also, during these two weeks the bridegroom has the job of calling personally on all those people he and his bride-to-be plan to invite to the wedding reception. In a large community such as ours, not everyone was "called" to weddings. Thus, it was quite an honor to be "called," especially to one being held in a neighboring church district within your settlement. Of course, all the relatives are "called" first. No "call" is official until the bridegroom has invited you personally. The mail may be used to invite people from a distant community. Anyone may attend the ceremony; however, you must be officially "called" to the wedding reception.

The uncles and aunts of the bride and bridegroom become the cooks for weddings. It is a special honor to be asked to cook since the Amish are traditionally known as great cooks. The cooks will appear at the future bride's house a couple of days before the wedding and begin baking pies, cakes, homemade noodles and so forth. A custom held in most Amish communities is for the bridegroom to kill the chickens for the wedding feast. Conspicuously absent in an Amish wedding or preplanning of the wedding is flowers and/or corsages of any type.

The bridegroom invites several of his close male friends or relatives to become the *hostlers*. These are the young men who help unhitch the guests' horses as they arrive. The wedding ceremony usually begins around nine o'clock in the morning and may last up until 1:00 p.m. or after. The service begins with the bride, usually dressed in a simple home sewn ankle length robin-egg blue dress, and bridegroom, dressed in black or dark gray, along with their attendants, meeting upstairs or in the basement with the bishops, deacons, and ministers of the church. During this time the congregation sings hymns. Although the attendants and the waiters are upstairs, they will not be in the same room with the couple to be married and the religious leaders. During the time the couple and the leaders are upstairs, they discuss the multifold responsibilities and obligations of an Amish Christian marriage.

Following an hour or so, the bishop, deacons and ministers, along with the couple and wedding party, resume their seats in front of the men in the living room of the house. One of the deacons delivers the initial sermon (in German) and refers often to Biblical references regarding the obligations of marriage. Following this initial sermon there are several minutes of kneeling in silent prayer. Then the bishop delivers the main wedding sermon. The wedding couple has nothing to say about the service. That is, nothing that happens will have been dictated by them. Also, the parents of both will have had little to say about the plans and are simply guests like others. The parents of neither will have been given any kind of special attention at the wedding or reception that follows.

Following the long wedding ceremony all those who had been given a "call" return to the home of the bride. Some who come bring a gift which may range from small pigs to saws or hammers for the bridegroom and cooking utensils and so forth for the bride. In many Amish communities names are not attached to gifts and no written "thank you" is expected.

After returning to the home of the bride the wedding party takes its place in a specially designed corner of the dining room. The tables will have been previously decorated with wedding cakes and other imaginative desserts. Usually these have been prepared by girlfriends of the bride or by the cooks. To be selected as a "carver" or a table waiter for a wedding is a distinct honor. There is always much speculation (some may say "gossip") as to who will be the carver and the waiters for an approaching wedding.

In some Amish communities it is a custom for the young unmarried men to form a group, pick up the bridegroom and toss him over the fence into the waiting arms of a group of young married men. Although this custom was not necessarily done at all the weddings in my community, I have witnessed it several times. This is called the expulsion of the "benedict." Symbolically, this is a transition from the carefree bachelorhood to the life of the Amish married man with the many related responsibilities.

Eating is an important activity of all present at the wedding. Eating occurs throughout the afternoon and usually up until 10:30 p.m. or midnight.

In most communities the young man and his wife will spend that night in an upstairs room at the bride's parents' home. There is nothing equivalent to a honeymoon in the Amish tradition. However, the newly married couple will spend the next couple of weeks visiting in the homes of their relatives. Here they will pick up additional practical gifts. Some Amish do refer to this as a type of honeymoon.

Following these few weeks of touring the Amish community, the couple will usually return to the home of the groom's father. They will spend some time here and wait for the opportunity to purchase land and/or take over one of the farms of one of their respective parents.

Few women or men remain single. The approximate age of marriage for men is 18 to 22 and for women is 18 to 21. Those women that do remain single cease attending the Sunday night singings (the "crowd") at about 25 or 26 years of age. They remain within the family orientation and usually take over some of the household and child-rearing duties of the mother. Often they work outside the Amish community as maids in local residences or become Amish school teachers. Frequently, these women will later marry older Amish widowers.

Remarriage, following the death of a spouse, is encouraged and is quite common one or two years following the death. The community is quite solicitous in this event and often makes suggestions to the widowed spouse for likely new partners.

I believe that the reader will gain much insight into the lives of young married Amish women of today by carefully reading the following letter which appeared in *Young Companion*.

Advice for the Young Married Woman

There are a number of tricks to make the old-fashioned way easier, more efficient and more enjoyable.

To begin with, people who have no other stove to cook with except a wood stove, heat their dishwater while they are cooking the meal. This way the fire is not needed for so long. Also, they use "summer" wood which burns quickly, heats well in the process, then dies out. Be sure to heat enough water to refill the dishpan if there are a lot of dishes. Washing dishes in cold water is not fun, and it does a poor job.

Once the meal is past, the dishes, pots, pans, platters and bowls are neatly stacked with the largest at the bottom. A cabinet top near the dry sink serves as counter space, and so does a deep window sill or a table.

Next, put the chunk of homemade soap in the dishpan and pour the hot water over it. (You should use rain water. Hard water doesn't work.) This will produce nice suds, especially if you're using a new chunk of soap. In fact, you will have to remove the soap before very long, or you will have far too many suds.

These suds are so different from detergent suds. Detergent suds are all on top. The suds of homemade soap are mixed in *and* on top of the water, making it nice and soft. Too many suds make the water slippery and slithery, or even slimy. I remember having to scoop suds out by the handful and still there were too many, all because I had left the soap in too long.

But when your chunk is old and small, you can pour hot water over it, swish all you like, and still get barely enough suds. Then it is time for a new chunk of soap.

An inbetween chunk of soap can be left in the water for a while, then removed for a turn, and when the suds grow fewer, put back into the water. Only don't forget to take the soap out before you dump the water. Otherwise, you will have to look for it in the grass and pick off any dirt and blades of grass that stick to it, or give it a good rinse under the pump.

If you have now done all the dishes, please wipe out the sink before you dump the water. You'll want to wring the "sink" water into the dishpan. And before you hang up the dishrag, rinse it in clean water. This will help to keep it from getting slippery.

When every dish has been put away, the sink is dry, the dishpan empty, and the dish rag hung up—how tidy the kitchen looks. And the dishpan can be used to snitz apples, scrub carrots, peel potatoes, you name it.

I'm not yet thirty-five, but I still prefer the old-fashioned way, especially homemade soap.

Anonymous—Reprinted from *Young Companion*

Death

Customs surrounding death and burial vary somewhat from one Amish community to another. Although quite young when she died, I feel that the following account of my own mother's death and burial as I remember it (with the help of my late father) is typical.

*   *   *   *   *

Mom had been complaining of a backache and stomach ache following the birth of my youngest brother. However, the advice of the physicians was sought too late and she died of a ruptured appendix.

My father explained to us children that we would not be seeing mom anymore because she had simply gone to sleep and that she was in heaven with God.

The family was in a quandary concerning a state law which required embalming. However, as dictated by law, the body was taken to a small Catholic funeral director where the embalming was performed. During this first evening the body remained at the funeral home. However, many of the neighbors, aunts, uncles and cousins came to our house making plans for my mom's funeral. News of the death spread quickly throughout our Amish settlement and all during that night relatives and non-relatives visited our home. Amish tradition prevailed and decisions regarding the funeral arrangements were made by relatives. Six of mom's nephews would serve as grave-diggers and pallbearers. Six non-relatives, three males and three females all past age sixteen but unmarried, would serve as the "chore boys and girls" who are customary when death claims an Amish sect participant. These people take over the farm chores and manage the household until two days following the funeral. These young people attend to their duties gladly since being chosen as a chore boy or girl is a sign of distinct maturity and a coveted responsibility among Amish youth.

Even though mom's body was still at the funeral home, the wake continued throughout the night. The chore boys and girls plus relatives and neighbors provided food which was served every six hours around the clock.

Another relative worked throughout the night building a casket—a simple pine box. There would be no concrete vault. The following morning the pine box was taken to the local funeral director and mom's body was then delivered to our house.

We were not confronted with typical decisions faced by the outsiders at such a grieving time. Tradition took care of these decisions. My mother was buried in a simple ceremony in an unmarked grave in an Amish cemetery. There were no flowers of any kind, no tent and no artificial grass at the burial site.

The chore group secured as many helpers as they needed for the preparation of the meals and our Amish neighbors delivered food to our home at all hours. Mom's funeral would be held on the third day following her death, traditional among the Amish.

The casket was placed in my parent's bedroom and a kerosene lamp remained lighted 24 hours a day. The light was dimly lit and I remember the erie shadows cast as people came in and out of the room to view the body. No one sat in this room, but from time to time people would get up from other rooms and walk into the bedroom, view the body and then quietly return to their sitting place in another part of the house. This was indeed a somber occasion.

On the second night of the wake it rained. I remember seeing the constant arrival and departure of dozens of black buggies. Our barnyard turned into a vast mudhole and since top-buggies were not permitted in my community at that time, there was little chance of avoiding the rain. The wet heavy shawls the women wore and the heavy serge material in the males' clothing had a distinct mothball odor when wet.

There were people in every room of our house and they talked in low voices and often visited the wooden casket. They sat around on low flat benches, brought in especially for funeral services, weddings and church services.

Early on the morning of the funeral the buggies began to arrive again. As the buggies arrived, the men and boys un-hitched the horses and tied them to a wooden fence around our barn lot. Women and children moved slowly toward the house which was gradually and quietly filling. The women hung their heavy black shawls and bonnets on the clothes line before enter-ing the house. Married men and small boys stopped to remove their overshoes on the porch and then filed in to take their places in the living room. The young, unmarried women (six-teen years of age or over) took their usual places behind these married men to the rear of the living room. The married women remained in the dining and kitchen area along with the younger children. The upstairs quickly filled with younger men and some older ones who had not found a place in the living room. Hundreds of people were left standing outside the house. They crowded close to the windows which by now had been opened slightly so as to hear the preaching services. The ministers, eight in all, were seated in front of the living room group facing the married men while the casket sat between the two groups. At 9:00 a.m. the first minister stood and began delivering a sermon such as one would hear on an ordinary Sunday at an Old Order Amish church service. He used this emotional occasion to plead with all the young people present to follow church (to follow church means to take instructions for six weeks and become a member if sixteen or beyond) and lead a life such as my mother had led. In about an hour, the second minister stood to preach the main sermon. His approach was also personal and direct. Several outsider friends of my mother were present and from time to time the ministers repeated themselves in English. Following about an hour of preaching, the second minister asked everyone to leave the living room so that the ministers could arrange the casket for the final viewing. The casket would not be opened at the grave site. At this point everyone returned to their seats and the third minister delivered a short obituary after which everyone kneeled for a long prayer. Then, all present formed a line and viewed mom for the last time. The men moved to the barnyard and began hitching their horses to the buggies and began lining up for the long trip to the Amish cemetery.

The hearse was one of our regular two-horse wagons with three spring- box type seats pushed forward. The casket was pushed into the wagon and, due to the three foot sideboards, was visible only to my family and me sitting in the seats above the casket. Dad told me that more than 100 buggies, pulled by horses in a narrow, curved line followed our hearse wagon that fateful day.

The cemetery, a small, plain field located in the midst of the Amish community, does not have gravestones such as are seen in modern cemeteries. Unaware outsiders do not realize that a cemetery is even located there.

Upon our arrival at the cemetery, the horses were left hitched to the buggies and were tied to the cemetery fence. The casket was moved to the grave and secured by two hickory poles placed over the grave site previously dug by six of my relatives. Following a few words by the bishop, the service ended and the gravediggers, using wide belt straps, lowered the casket into the ground. One man descended into the grave and taking shovelfuls of dirt from above handed to him by other gravediggers, gently and slowly placed dirt on the casket. After the casket was covered with a thin layer of dirt, the man left the hole in the ground to join the other gravediggers who quickly filled the grave. At this point everyone turned to leave the grave for the journey back to our home where all again would eat.

The only outsider present at the grave side services was the undertaker. I remember as we were slowly making our way back to my home how the undertaker's black car sped past our buggies. Today, I think about how out-of-place an automobile was on such a sad day for my family.

As we left the cemetery, my father told his family that there would be no reason for us to return to my mother's resting place. She was no longer there, and I have never returned.

Back at our house the community waited for the post-funeral meal. Everyone contributed. There was a large granite bowl of mashed potatoes, fried chicken, a crock of sauerkraut cooked in pork broth, noodles, apple pie and plenty of coffee.

The next day my household returned to normality. The grief was not easy; however, it had been made lighter because the entire community had shared it with us. The Amish community always shares the grief of one of its members, whether it be the loss of a loved one through death or through expulsion from the community.

Section VI

The Amish Plan of Education

By now it should be obvious to the reader that Amish young-sters are raised very carefully and that rigorous methods are employed to protect them from the contaminating influences of the outsider. And, this is especially true regarding education. If there is a fear among Amish parents, it is the fear of their youth obtaining too much formal education. Formal education, to the Amish, ends with the eighth grade.

A Brief History of the Problems with Public Schools

The Amish are opposed to any formal education beyond the eighth grade, and for most, below that level if it requires attend-ing a modern, consolidated public school. They are opposed especially to the emphasis placed on science, the competitive atmosphere and the alien "outsider" teachers found there. They prefer the old-fashioned, one- or two-room school with its lim-ited facilities, in as much as this type of school is more in keep-

ing with the simple life at home. Although many Amish communities have some type of vocational school for those beyond
the eighth grade but not yet of legal quitting age, most prefer to
train their youth at home in matters dealing with the care and
operation of farms and farm households.

Contrary to popular belief, Old Order Amish schools in the US
are on the increase in the new millennium. Historically, this growth
has been phenomenal and is expected to continue at a rapid rate
over the next several years. For example, the 1972 *Amish Teacher
Directory* listed the names and addresses of only **329** Amish schools
in the US with around 5,000 students enrolled. This same directory
also listed the founding date of each school and more than 90% of
those had been founded since 1968! In 1990 there were **719** Old
Order Amish schools in the US, a growth of 100% in only twenty
years, with approximately 20,000 students enrolled in grades one
through eight. Today there are more than 500 Old Order Amish
schools scattered across 26 states, with an enrollment of more than
35,000 one through eight grade students. *Amazingly, this is an
increase of more than 40% since 1990!* There were 720 teachers in 1990
while in 2005 the number has *more than doubled!* Holmes County,
Ohio alone has 145 one or two room Amish schools (USA Today,
April 15, 2005).

The teachers in the Amish Schools are Old Order Amish, eight
grade graduates and not "teacher" certified, per se, by the states in
which they teach. An overwhelming majority of the teachers are
female. The average student (students are called "scholars") per
teacher ratio in the Amish schools nationwide in the 2000—2001
school year was 19.2, a ratio to be envied by public school teachers.

Although there are still a few Old Order Amish children
attending public elementary schools today, the numbers are small
and decreasing every year. The extension of the school year by
public school authorities upset the Amish since this interfered with
the Amish practice of having the children help with the farming.
This school year extension, the banning of prayers in the public
school, the emphasis on science and evolution, the increase of gun
violence and drug usage in America, educational television and
computer technology are among the major factors that resulted in
Amish children's mass exodus from the public schools. Amish
parents contend that, according to the *Bible*, their children belong to
them and thus are not to be educated by the state nor for the benefit

of the state. Anything taught beyond the three Rs is a waste of time. Educational television, school pictures, competitive sports, gym classes with scanty uniforms and pledges of allegiance are among the many "Godless" features banned from the Amish schools.

The Amish adults realize that public school teachers strive to instill a love of learning in their charges. And, when Amish children do attend public schools, they are good, obedient, hard-working students, and well-liked by their teachers. These teachers, out of compassion, often impose their values on Amish children and strive to alter their perceptions of life. Admittedly, this is usually an unconscious effort on the part of the teacher, but its intent is just as deadly to the Amish way of life. Compassionate non-Amish individuals such as teachers often look upon the Amish youth as deprived and thus try to be "helpful," but are often harmful.

I can vouch for the dissonance and psychological pain endured by Amish youth in a public elementary school. One who has never been a member of a distinct minority group surrounded by the majority can ever fully realize the notion of being "different." The two forces—the internalized Amish values and the dominant culture's values—antagonize one another constantly. Put yourself in the Amish child's place in the following school situations: 1) The non-Amish children in the class see an educational film with the teacher's assurance that it is worthwhile and educational; however, you have been taught that it is sinful to view any film and you leave the room so as not to be contaminated. 2) You are told by the teacher that it is truly American to salute the flag and to pledge allegiance, but as the other children stand to do so, you must remain seated because the *Bible* says, "Have no other Gods before me." 3) Your teacher indicates that fighting for your country is American and the non-Amish youth are constantly talking about what branch of the service they will someday join; however, you realize that as a conscientious objector, you will never go to war. 4) As an assignment, you are to talk about your favorite cartoon character, but you have never seen a television set and your parents do not subscribe to the daily newspaper. And, (5) your first language is German and you are constantly reminded to speak English. Literally dozens of similar situations could be cited. Thus, it is no wonder that Amish children, as indicated below, are leery of non-Amish schools and **"glad I go to our school."**

No Public School for Me

In public school they teach worldly stuff that isn't good for Amish children. I once talked to an English girl and she told me they see picture shows and cartoons in school. She told me about one picture show about a haunted house. It was scary just hearing her tell it. I'm glad I go to our school....

Ruth, fifth grade

In addition to the above, Amish parents are especially concerned about the consequences of their offspring's association with the "outsider" children in the public school. The parents realize that their children would acquire needs which cannot be satisfactorily fulfilled within the confines of the Amish culture.

The average American school is especially congruent with middle-class attitudes and the teachers' main objective is to transmit this cultural heritage to American youth. This objective frightens the God-fearing Amish who do not want their children attaining, nor even being exposed to, many of today's American values. They fear that modern education overemphasizes science, technology and violence.

The Amish always have opposed sending their children to the public high schools, but many Amish were not that opposed to the public elementary schools until the late sixties and early seventies. The Amish leaders realized at that time in their history that the sect's survival was at stake if their youth continued to attend any type of public school, and they took action to stop the practice. They believed, as they do today, that the education obtained there was irrelevant and would only alienate the Amish children against their culture and parents. Thus, they began to develop their own schools with a curriculum (and surroundings) they felt would best meet the needs of the Amish society. These schools, developed in each of the twenty states then inhabited by the Old Order Amish, ran into difficulty with the state and local educational authorities in most every state. A major confrontation resulted between the Amish and the educational authorities because of the Amish sect's desire to employ their own eighth-grade graduates as teachers. However, the biggest and most threatening problem with the state and local school authorities focused on Amish children who were beyond the eighth grade but not yet of legal quitting age. The Amish felt these children should be considered finished with their formal education. However, they were being forced to go to high school until they were of legal quitting age. The Amish usually do not balk at rules and laws unless they are very opposed to them. And, they were very much opposed to sending their children on to high school and many, many Amish parents served jail sentences as a result.

To this writer there was no doubt that America's emphasis on education in the late sixties and early seventies, especially high school education, was threatening the Old Order Amish sect's values and way of life. And, I knew that something had to change or (in my opinion) the Amish would disappear from America. The nonconforming Amish were having difficulty with several innovative aspects of the dominant American society that surrounded them at that time in their history; however, none seemed as insurmountable as their predicament regarding modern, compulsory high school attendance for their youth. This unwanted education being imposed on them was causing many Amish youth to leave the sect and many Amish families to leave America in search of religious freedom!

Literally hundreds of cases of Amish parents being fined and/or placed in jail for refusing to send their children to high school could be documented. There are even documented cases of Amish children being legally taken from their parents, placed in children's homes and forced to attend high school. In another highly publicized case, Amish children were forced into school buses by sheriff's deputies and driven to a local high school. Then, on May 15, 1972 a dramatic event occurred—the *National Committee for Amish Freedom*, on behalf of the Amish, won a unanimous U.S. Supreme Court decision exempting them from state laws compelling their children to continue schooling beyond the eighth grade. In essence, the court indicated that compulsory, formal education beyond the eighth grade would greatly endanger, if not destroy, free exercise of the Amish religious beliefs.

The ruling affirmed a 1971 judgment by the Wisconsin Supreme Court, first in the country to protect the Amish from school attendance laws. Legal scholars indicate that this is the first time in the history of America that compulsory education laws have been successfully challenged. And, to this date, no other group has been successful in this regard.

The case involved three Wisconsin Amish fathers who were fined a symbolic five dollars each for refusing to enroll their adolescent children in the local public high school.

The Supreme Court ruling meant that the Amish, who had always considered formal education past the eighth grade to be sinful, could no longer be forced by any state authorities to continue schooling beyond that level.

As the then vice-chairman of the National Committee for Amish Religious Freedom, the organization defending the "defenseless Christian" in this battle, and as a former member of the Old Order Amish sect, I was personally relieved and gratified by the ruling. Having grown up Amish for the first sixteen years of my life, I found it hard to realize that day in 1972 that this conflict was finally over. I remember well the turmoil in my community each time an Amish child, beyond eighth grade but not of legal quitting age, was forced into high school. Some of the Amish leaders had worked out an agreement with local public school teachers so that Amish children would purposely be failed in the eighth grade and thus would repeat the grade until they were of legal quitting age. Other parents, including mine, held their children out of elementary school until age eight so that they would be sixteen (the legal quitting age in most states) upon completion and never enter the local, contaminating high school. The local school authorities usually "winked" at this practice and seldom forced the issue.

In retrospect, it has always been clear to me that the American high school could in no way transmit the values needed by an Amish youth to remain Amish. The public high school generally prepares its students for college, whereas the post elementary education plan proposed by the Amish prepares their children for Amishhood, for life as God-fearing Amish people. The Supreme Court decision made this possible.

The Amish Schools Today

Following the Supreme Court decision, the Amish reached agreements with the state school authorities in every state in which they lived. Some states agreed to a high school equivalent education for all their Amish parochial school teachers. This high school education requirement is met by taking the high school equivalent General Educational Development (GED) test and obtaining a minimum score set by the respective state. The first of these tests, administered by the writer and State of Indiana educational officials, were given to over 70 Old Order Amish males and females and yielded some of the highest scores ever recorded for the GED in Indiana. More than 75% passed the first examination and were then qualified to teach in the Amish schools. Some of those taking the tests were as young as sixteen; others were beyond sixty years of age.

Each Amish community elects an all male school board and several states have elected state level executive school boards, also all male. None of these officials will have graduated from high school. The local boards literally run their local school and their word is final. And, it is their duty to see to it that the teacher is doing a good job. Board members often visit the school when in session and take their job very seriously.

The Amish have agreed to two semesters of instruction in reading, writing, spelling and arithmetic. A minimum of one semester of instruction is taught each year in both geography and history. All courses must be taught utilizing the English language. German, the Amish child's first language, may be taught as a subject at the option of the local school board. In many Amish schools one afternoon a week is set aside for German lessons taught with the help of interested parents (The writer was present during one of these community instruction periods and observed ten parents instructing 31 students). Science, art, shop and organized physical education are not a part of the curriculum and there are few extracurricular activities. No textbooks are used except those recommended by the Amish school boards and many are hand-me-downs from the local public school system. Some Amish elders and others, will, from time to time, suggest that the teachers use only German in all instruction. However, I know of no Amish school where this occurs. The Amish realize that they must do business with their non-Amish, English speaking neighbors and that they must, as stated in the following essay, "**teach English**."

We Must Teach English

We live in an English speaking country. Our textbooks are printed in English. The English language is very much a part of our surroundings. Most parents learned it in public school, but where will our children learn it? They will have to learn it, too, in school—parochial school. And the best way for them to learn it is to have them speak it. Learning a language takes practice, and eight years in parochial school is a good place to practice. The result should be that by graduation the children will have a good enough command of English to be able to deal sufficiently with the society around them.

Once the teacher has the backing of her school board and parents for an "English at all times" rule, one problem yet remains—how to enforce it. Perhaps the solution is to grade. Children are graded in written English grammar, why not also grade them for their ability to speak correctly? Somewhere on the report cards the teacher should type ENGLISH (spoken) and place a mark there each grading period. Not only should children receive a grade for their ability to use English in conversation during classtime, a teacher could even make tests which the pupils would answer, not in writing, but orally. In this way she will be able to determine the student's ability to handle English.

Text books, bankers, salesmen, neighbors, newspapers—our surroundings are filled with English. In some situations a reading ability is needed, in others a writing ability, and others a speaking ability. All three—reading, writing and speaking—go hand in hand in learning a language. With a little extra effort our parochial schools will have the proper balance.

Anonymous—Reprinted from *Blackboard Bulletin*

After successfully completing the eighth grade, and not having reached the age of sixteen, pupils in some Amish school systems enroll in the vocational division. In some systems the vocational students attend school at least one day (five hours) per week during the regular school year until legal quitting age, usually fifteen or sixteen. During this didactic experience they discuss their vocational projects and attend classes in history, general business, mathematics, English and spelling. I am familiar with one system where the vocational students are required to work a minimum of four hours a day on their projects when not in school. Much of the obligation for the vocational plan is put upon the shoulders of the Amish parents. Parents are involved deeply with their school and often visit the premises. The writer was present at an annual state-wide all day school meeting where over 200 Amish adults, mostly men, were in attendance. This number may not seem in excess; however, if one considers that the meeting was held on a weekday during the hay season and that the adults had to come long distances in horse-drawn buggies, it is amazing!

The vocational project areas usually include livestock and poultry, fruits and vegetables, grains, tools, horse-drawn farm equipment, carpentry, homemaking, gardening and so forth. All projects are in regard to the farm and home. However, in some systems, services outside the home may be classified as projects if done in cooperation with neighbors, after obtaining the consent of the parents and the vocational instructor. The projects are supervised by the vocational teacher from beginning to end and it is emphasized that daily chores and routine household duties are not to be considered as vocational projects. Parents are required to keep tabs on the progress of projects and must sign all reports turned in by their respective vocational students.

The Amish educational methods are valid in that they fulfill the needs of the Amish culture. If education is judged by its achievements, the Amish may have one of the most effective instructional systems in the world today. And, the Amish vocational school is itself a major adaption, the first formalized instruction beyond the eighth grade the Old Order Amish have ever been willing to accept. And, it works for them!

The writer has visited many of the Amish parochial schools and has spent several hours in observation of Amish teachers. Previous to the development of their schools, all Amish were farmers and/or farmers' wives; thus, the Amish teachers place great value on teaching as an occupation and on their ability to teach writing, reading and arithmetic. Teachers are held in high esteem and it is an honor to be a teacher. Admittedly, these teachers have not gone beyond the eighth grade formally, but to categorize them as high school "dropouts" would be unjustifiable and a misnomer. They are grounded fully in the Amish doctrines, and are selected because of their spiritual well-being, resourcefulness, efficiency, and especially, their motivation. Many of the Amish teachers receive the equivalent of a high school diploma via correspondence schools. In this manner of educating themselves, they retain their basic philosophy of remaining *"apart from the world."*

Anyone visiting the Amish schools will observe efficient teaching methods being utilized and true learning taking place in the absence of technology, a red pencil and a B.S. degree! The Amish teachers teach reading, writing and arithmetic with tender loving care. These teachers, because of the familial and cultural training received, refrain from harsh, coercive methods and use group praise abundantly. Their cultural background predetermines non-aggressiveness, and the assertive, punitive approach to education is not observed in the Amish schools. The teacher and "scholars"—as Amish pupils are referred to—are on a first name basis, and are often related. Modern educators who learn of this often reveal their amazement at such mannerisms and are concerned about respect and discipline. However, Amish teachers have few disciplinary problems with their "scholars."

The basic reason for the absence of serious discipline problems is the children's respect for authority, the real involvement of the parents and the Amish instructor's belief that they are guides, rather than teachers, in the formation of the Amish child's life.

———————▶ ● ◀———————

My Teacher

...I like Mary, our teacher. She is nice, kind and a Christian. I went to school with the English my first two years and didn't like it. They were so loud and my first teacher was loud too. She had her fingers painted and her lips were very red. She scared me one day. I like Mary best. She is my cousin....

Rebecca, fourth grade

———————▶ ● ◀———————

There is a conspicuous absence of the critical and analytical methods of teaching in the Amish schools and memorization is the major learning technique utilized. The Amish society is such that few things are written (seldom even the rules of the church) and the Amish teachers realize the importance of memorization to a participant of such an oral-traditional culture. They teach their charges to be mild, unquestioning, nonaggressive and obedient. They do not foster the development of creativity nor innovativeness.

Most of the Amish schools utilize two academic teachers— one for grades one through four and another for grades five through eight. The teachers often have teaching aides and utilize the older students in tutoring roles extensively. The teaching salary, paid from an assessment of the Amish church members, varies from $15 to $20 per day and may include payment for the janitorial chores which often accompany the teaching duties. Both male and female teachers could make considerably more money if employed elsewhere. Females working as "maids" for outsiders make more money than do the Amish teachers. And, the same can be stated for Amish male carpenters. Teachers obviously love their work.

The following excerpts, taken from an issue of the *Blackboard Bulletin*, are statements made at an Amish Midwestern School Meeting.

———————●————————

"Show your teacher your appreciation. Give her a raise at mid-term."

"Killing a mosquito with a sledge hammer gets an overkill."

"God likes small people—He cannot use big ones."

"I shoe horses for a living. It's hard work, but I would not shoe horses for the wages a teacher gets."

"With slow learners, tell them what you are going to say, then say it, then tell them what you said."

"All good things go to ruin if we don't work on them."

"The effort to catch the foxes that ruin our schools begins within ourselves. We cannot catch our neighbor's foxes."

"We can't teach a dog anything unless we know more than the dog."

"Teachers are human, and humans all have something in common—they at times have a problem with the capital letter 'I'."

"The electric chair is not the solution to crime, but the high chair."

"Our schools cannot be better than the homes the children come from."

"School is like a threshing machine; one small part can disrupt the function of the whole works."

Anonymous—Reprinted from the *Blackboard Bulletin*

———————●————————

Amish schools are built within 3-4 miles of one another so that the "scholars" can easily walk or drive a horse and buggy to school.

The school building generally is rectangular in shape and constructed of wood framing covered with clapboard. There is a cupola at the entrance, followed by two sex-separated anterooms for garment hanging. Once inside the main room, one normally sees simple drawings of animals, fruits and vegetables, along with

Bible verses and aphorisms decorating the walls. The students sit at desks which, in many cases, have been discarded from a public school classroom. There are neither window curtains nor electric lights, and a potbellied stove adorns a corner of the room. It is evident that the physical aspects of the school, along with the curriculum, coincide with the Amish values and ways.

Many comments, some rather strongly worded, have been made by educational experts regarding the use of eighth-grade graduates as Amish teachers. Educational authorities often believe that these teachers are inadequate and that the Amish students will not learn. However, it is my professional opinion that the Amish school system works. The teachers take their jobs seriously and do a good job. And, the Amish schools are teaching what Amish parents want their children to know and learn. The tenacious Amish utilize their schools to maintain their cultural integrity and uniqueness as a minority group. I sincerely believe that if the Amish had not been permitted their own schools, they would have become extinct to America in a short time.

Grace Miller, after visiting an Amish school, wrote a small piece titled: *The ABC,s of an Amish School* **(amish-heartland.com, September 26, 2005).** Miller indicated that her visit was like being transported back in time to a school in the middle of the last century or even before. She stated that she observed, *"Rows of wooden desks facing a long blackboard flanked by cork bulletin boards. The alphabet letters, capital and lower-case, march high around the walls of the room, illustrating proper penmanship, as well as prompting beginning readers. A world globe sits atop a bookcase crammed with books. Roll-up maps hang ready for a geography lesson about the continents. A village constructed in cardboard by the sixth, seventh and eighth-grade boys is displayed on a shelf at the back of the room, just over the hooks where the youngsters hang their coats and lunch pails."*

Although the Amish do not extend their formal schooling beyond the eighth grade, it would be a mistake to think the gentle people do not value education. Amish leaders understand the importance, especially economically, of learning and understanding all they can about the "English" society. They know that they must peacefully co-exist with the "world" if they are to survive. Although most Amish children enter school speaking only Pennsylvania Dutch, the Amish adults also realize the importance of becoming proficient in both speaking and writing the English language. And, upon graduation from the eighth grade, all Amish children enter a vocational school. In essence, **all of Amish society becomes the "vocational school"** for the eighth grade graduates.

Miller stated: *"The primary purpose of their grade one through eight grade schools is to provide a solid grounding in the basics, producing scholars who can read, write, spell and do arithmetic competently. There are no frills in this classroom, but everything needed for a basic education is provided, paid for entirely by the tuition fee charged to parents, as well as much volunteer labor, donated land and the cooperative efforts of the Amish community at large."*

Miller was impressed with the efficiency of the classroom she visited and wrote, *"Amish scholars pack a lot of learning into their eight years in school. With their well-known frugality, the Amish also wring a lot of education from relatively few dollars."*

In this non-electric environment, there are no expensive computers, televisions, or other electronic equipment. The Amish "scholars" bring their lunches to school daily, thus eliminating the need for kitchen and cafeteria facilities. And all "physical education" classes are conducted informally on the playground outside during noon recess in various, high-energy running games.

More could be written about the Amish plan of education and more reasons could be given, both by myself and the Amish, concerning the positive aspects of the Supreme Court's decision permitting the Amish to have their own unique plan of education. What does it mean? It means the Amish with their unique ways can remain unique. It is not only legitimate now to be an Amishman in America, it is also legitimate to be educated as one. Many Amish people left America because of persecution and cited the school problem as a basic reason for their departure. But, the court decision stopped the Amish exodus to Central and South America.

Section VII

Problems in the New Millennium

———————●———————

The New Road

We now have a new blacktop road that replaced the gravel road through our settlement and lots of people I know are upset by it. The English built the road so they could connect up the two towns of _____ and _____. My Dad says that it will only bring faster, more dangerous cars and tourists with cameras out here that will try to take pictures of us. My older sister said once that if they try to take your picture that you should just stick your tongue out—not at them—but at the ground or the sky. My Dad is worried about what the hard blacktop will do to our horses. He said that a driving horse is good for 10 years or more if you pull your buggy on gravel or dirt roads. But, if you drive the horse on blacktop you will hurt his legs and he won't last more than a few years for buggy pulling. I don't know why they had to bring the new road right through the community. I'm scared that we will just be having more buggy wrecks now with the fast cars hitting us...

Jonas, eighth grade

———————●———————

Problems Facing the Amish in the New Century

How long will civilization go along with the Old Order Amish? How long can the Amish with their closed society housed within a highly progressive, technologically driven society survive? Will the values, moral codes, principles and standards they adhere to disappear? Or worse, will the Amish lose so many of their youth to the "outside world" that they will simply disappear as a sub-population in America?

In my opinion, the answer to both of the latter questions is a definite "no." Matter of fact, it has been documented elsewhere in this book that the Old Order Amish are increasing in number rather dramatically in America. One of the best indicators of this tremendous growth was given in the last section of this book concerning their schools. There I reported a 40% increase of both Amish students and US Amish schools since 1990! And, such growth in the Amish population is expected to continue at the same pace, or perhaps even increase, over the next several years. As you will observe in my comments below, I am also convinced beyond doubt that the standards, values and principles the Amish follow will also remain basically intact.

However, whether the Amish can maintain their values and way of life is being questioned by sociologists and other experts who have studied and written about the Amish. These experts pose such dire questions as; will the Amish even survive as a culture in America? If they do survive, can they maintain and enhance the values, standards, moral codes and principles they cherish? That is, can they survive as they currently exist while remaining so distinctly different from the mainstream culture surrounding them? As noted, it is my belief that the Amish will not only survive as a culture but that they will also maintain their current values and distinctiveness as long as they can keep the figurative wall between themselves and the secular, *"worldly"* society. They have done this very well, under tremendous odds, for the past three centuries and I see no reason why their survival as a distinct culture is at risk for extinction. But, in all honesty, maintaining this figurative "wall" is becoming more difficult day by day for the Amish. And, unfortunately, failure to maintain this separation from the *"world"* brought about the disappearance of the Amish in Europe and I suppose the same could occur in America. However, again, I believe this to be a very remote possibility.

Are the Amish changing at all? Yes, the Amish are facing several things in the new millennium that are bringing changes to their culture, especially in their methods of making a living.

Urbanization and the Amish Farmer

The Amish have, since the sect's founding, been an agrarian people deeply committed to farming and have historically been viewed by non-Amish as exceptional farmers. That is, non-Amish agricultural experts have long marveled at the Amish people's non-exploitation of the earth in their farming methods. And, in their own way, the Amish have always been, and still are, strict environmentalists. They have a trusting relationship with the earth and believe that it is their duty to take care of "God's earth." When I was growing up a favorite uncle would often pick up a handful of soil, look at it with great respect while letting it slip through his fingers, and solemnly say: "You can't get much closer to God than this!"

Up until just a few years ago, all Amish youth knew they were either going to be a farmer or a farmer's wife as adults and career planning was not something that concerned them. Their lives were planned for them from birth to death as farming has always been their main occupation and source of income. However, it is estimated that less than 50% of the Old Order Amish in the US base their current livelihood solely on farming. Farming is no longer the expected sole occupation for the Amish.

What has caused such a drastic change from just a few years ago when practically all Old Order Amish where farmers? Simply put, urbanization has, and will continue, to threaten the horse farming practices as the Amish have known them for the past two plus centuries. This change will occur even more rapidly as farming becomes more mechanized and real estate developments send up the price of land across the US. This very visible threat has many Amish farmers switching from farming to various other church approved occupations.

Specific Farming Related Issues

The economic problems of farming people committed to a primitive technology, but imbedded in a highly technological society with which it must make exchanges across system lines, are immeasurable. They reject the use of modern chemistry methods,

---

biotechnology, and genetic engineering in any of their farming practices. They view all these as counter to the *Bible* and ecologically irresponsible.

There are many issues and problems facing the Amish farmer in the twenty-first Century. For example, one of the Amish farmer's largest economic supplements for many years has been the selling of fluid milk to local dairies. Now, new laws and demands of milk inspectors have made it difficult for the Amish to continue to sell milk to the dairies. Many Old Order Amish farmers have gone along with the new type milk parlors and gasoline engine operated cooling systems now required, but the notion of milking machines, for example, is not compatible with the Amish belief in non-conformity. But, many milk buyers no longer buy milk that has been produced by "hand." Further, the Amish have continually refused to allow their milk to be picked up on Sunday and dairies want the Amish farmer's milk seven days a week or not all. Many Amish now use Sunday's milk to make cheese for sale to others and "Amish cheese" has become the rage among tourists visiting the Amish areas.

The horse farming Amish are also at a distinct disadvantage, in many ways, when compared to their non-Amish farming neighbors. For example, they spurn any and all government entitlements, as they are opposed to government handouts and subsidies. This principle makes it even more difficult to compete with their non-Amish neighbors who readily accept farm-related entitlements.

Another advantage the outsider farmers have on the Amish farmer is their use of artificial insemination for breeding farm animals. The Amish understand the advantages of such worldly things as artificial insemination for breeding, but would never use such "ungodly" practices. This would be unnatural and counter to God's natural way of reproduction.

As of this writing another problem is looming for the Amish farmer, especially in Lancaster County Pennsylvania. Environmentalists there are becoming concerned that the manure produced by the Amish cattle herds are penetrating the groundwater level and endangering the drinking water in that part of the US. Rain carries it into the rivers and streams and is causing the fish to die, or so say the environmentalists. The government wants to restrict the Amish to one cow for every two acres of land, which would devastate the

Amish farmer. In addition, scientists have written that cows also belch off large amounts of methane gas harmful to the ozone layer and that their numbers should be restricted per farmer. To say the least, the Amish feel challenged and confused about this concern and do not understand why the "world" is suddenly so upset with them and their cattle.

There are many things that cause friction between the Amish farmer and his non-Amish farming neighbor. One of these concerns rumors regarding the Amish and taxes. Contrary to persistent rumors, the Amish are exempt from only Social Security tax, but they also do not receive the benefits. Amish employers also do not pay workers' compensation insurance for their Amish employees. The church does not believe in such insurance and steps in and takes care of their own if and when injuries do occur. Amish employers do, however, have to cover non-Amish workers with these fringe benefits. Many other false assumptions about the Amish that cause friction between them and their non-Amish farming neighbors could be given here.

Small Acreage "Farms"

As noted above, as we enter the new millennium many Amish are having to turn away from farming for their livelihood and at least half of them have practically given up farming. Many will have sold their main farm and/or have divided it among their adult, married children and will have then themselves gone into careers other than farming. In many Amish communities one can observe several generations now living on the original farm place and the men, and some of the women, being employed in jobs away from the farm and home.

It is commonplace in Amish communities today for the parents 100 acre farm, for example, to have been divided into ten or so 5 or 10 acre plots and then given to their offspring. Each will have built a home, a small barn and a few buildings on their plot of land. And, since they cannot make their living solely by farming such small acreage, many of the families will have gone full time into home based businesses and/or traditionally approved occupations of masonry and carpentry, building homes and furniture for the "outsider" etc. Many are also now working in church-approved, non-union factories.

Interestingly, when you ask a non-farming Amish man about his occupation, he will still mention farming first. And the fact is every Old Order Amish family does live on a farm of sorts. As noted, those Amish families who no longer farm for their only source of income will still own enough acreage for a large garden and a pasture area for their buggy horses to graze. In addition, most will also own a couple of hundred chickens, a few cows to milk twice a day for personal use, a few pigs for butchering purposes, etc. The Amish believe strongly that some type of farm life is still the best way for the children to learn responsibility. Thus, whether on a small plot of land or a large farm, the Amish offspring will be required to take care of the chickens, the few pigs, the milk cows, the buggy horses and, along with their mothers, the garden. The Amish believe that their families should "eat out of the garden and not out of the store."

Amish adults are adamant that simply because they no longer own large farms does not mean, or in any way justifies, that their children have fewer responsibilities than when sect members where full time farmers. As an Amish cousin who now builds fancy carriages for cities to use to transport visiting tourists told me, **"The children still get up at 5 AM every morning, light the lantern and do their chores."** He went on to state with a twinkle in his eye, **"The** *Bible* **says that if you don't work you don't eat so they have to work for their breakfast."** Of course, this also helps the children face the realities of their ongoing responsibilities into Amish adulthood.

Amish Farmers

...I think that Amish men are good farmers. Although we should not brag or show pride, I do believe we do things maybe a little bit better than the outsider farmer does that is good for God's land. We are different and we also farm in a different way. We use horses to farm for good reasons. My dad has a saying about horses that I like. He says, "Horses reproduce but tractors produce debts and pollution." We don't run tractors over a wet field and make big hard dirt clods that won't break up till next Spring. That's not good for God's earth...

Paul, seventh grade

The Amish settlements most threatened by urbanization are those that are close to large metropolitan areas. However, Amish communities are faced with the spread of urban life from even smaller cities. As noted, land prices have skyrocketed and Amish farmers will sometimes out-bid their non-Amish neighbors for land within, or near a traditional Amish settlement. However, a half million dollars or more is much more money than the Amish can afford to pay for a farm. Thus, the amount of acreage considered necessary for making a living at general farming is now out of reach for many Amish trying to get started in the farming business. In some areas, Amish are cooperating to buy farms by providing each other interest free loans. And in response, more and more "outsider" farm auctions are being held on Sunday, eliminating the cooperative Amish bidders. Thus, as noted above, many Amish farm owners have found themselves dividing their acreage into much smaller plots and taking jobs in industry and/or are starting their own home-based enterprises.

Industrial work is a departure from tradition made necessary by the changing economy. Factory hours are shorter and pay checks are higher. In time factory work will no doubt erode some of the values the Amish have so long treasured. Factory work is especially detrimental to the close knit Amish family organization. It is obvious from the following excerpts from letters (written by Amish mothers) to *Family Life* that the Amish realize this deterioration better than anyone.

———————•———————

Factory Work

...How can a father fulfill his duty when he is away from home all day? My husband worked in a factory for three years and I can see now where he and the oldest boy lost out on a father and son basis by having the boy farming alone mostly. He was too young for such a responsibility. Of course, I tried to help him along as best I could but with other children to care for, he was left alone too much of the time. Now that he is older, he has gone on his own. Please be patient for your boys need your love and fatherly help while they are young. Before you realize it they will be big enough to help and then things will go better....

———————●———————

...Don't you think you can live a closer life to God on the farm? I'm afraid the factories are leading good men farther and farther away from God. Which is the more important, money or a soul? Would you not rather lose everything you have than to lose your soul? And how about the precious souls of your boys?

———————●———————

...I would like to add a word of warning to the fathers who are working away day after day and are not at home with their family. They are not teaching their sons how to work so how will these sons learn to like to work when they grow up? What will it come to? If their sons don't learn to work while young, they will grow up and when they have a family of their own it's the family that will have to suffer. If the head of the family has to push himself to work, there will scarcely be enough to supply his family, let alone all the things his father didn't teach him to do. How can he teach his sons?

Anonymous—All reprinted from *Family Life*

———————●———————

Some Amish churches that changed their "orders" permitting factory work have been known to reverse that decision just as quickly, maybe even the following Sunday! And, many outsider factory owners are perplexed when, because of a new rule made on the previous Sunday, not one of their hard-working Amish men shows up for work on Monday morning!

As noted above, urbanization and progress has brought about a change for many Amish men. However, it is also changing the lifestyles of many Amish females. There have always been a few young men leaving the Amish church, but now some young women are following suit. In the past, a woman leaving the Amish church was almost unheard of. Why this sudden shift? Most Amish elders blame it on "working out" in modern outsider's homes or in factories. When young women work for another Amish family, they earn between $40.00 and $60.00 a week. However, they learn quickly that they can earn the same amount in one day by doing housework or factory work in town.

Losing a member to the outside world causes tremendous grief for the person's family, the church and other members of the community. The following letter in *Family Life* entitled "**One is a Big Number,**" depicts just how great the grief can be.

———➤●◄———

One Is Indeed Big

After reading the article, "One Is A Big Number" (July), I felt moved to share our experience. As parents of a large family, we have also felt the loss of a son, only in a different way. Yes, one space is empty. The shirt and the shoes are still here—abandoned for worldly clothes. Ah, yes, in the quietness of a summer's night one hears a car roaring in the distance. It might be him. We also cry, "Oh, God, all the pleading admonitions, the prayers, are they all in vain? Can such a sorrow also bring joy?"

Through earnest prayer we have obtained peace, but are still struggling. Yes, one is a big number.

Anonymous—Reprinted from *Family Life*

———➤●◄———

Even though some Amish people may enjoy working in factories, they find many requirements there that are contrary to their religion. For example, many industries require that their workers be unionized. This is strictly forbidden by Old Order Amish church rules and is causing tremendous conflict for many Amish people and factory owners alike. Although this may sound trivial, a very important aspect of an Amishman's garb is his black felt hat. This black hat is an important symbol of his religion. However, in many factories Amish men are required to wear hard hats. The church forbids this and Amish men have lost their jobs as a result.

Young Amish women are also "working out" in record numbers. And, as an Amish person wrote, **"I think it would be a good standard not to allow such outside jobs."**

A Finger in the Fire

I was thankful to see the story, "The Path of Temptation." The message is much needed, especially in a community where many girls work out for "English" people. Some may think the girls can be a good influence on their employers, but it usually turns out the other way—usually the young person is the one to be influenced, and not for good. They may soon see no harm in Christian radio programs, even though so-called Christian rock music and hymns, and truth and falsehood are mixed and aired. If you put your finger to the fire, it will get burnt. From experience, I know the evils of TV are very great. No mother in her right mind would let her young daughter take a baby-sitting job if she knew what temptations and evils the girl may be faced with daily.

Also, when you walk into an Amish home you can often detect if the girls (or even the mother, in earlier years) have worked in a worldly home, just by observing how the house is dolled up. Also, such girls often tend to be fence crowders in church. So overall, I think it would be a good standard to not allow such outside jobs. Or at least get the church's consent before making an exception.

Anonymous—Reprinted from *Young Companion*

Except for the nicknamed "Yellow Buggy" Amish and Nebraska Amish (both groups are found in Pennsylvania) whose buggies are brown with white tops, all Amish buggies are either pitch black or gray. Some Old Order Amish churches also permit tops on their buggies while others do not. However, the three-cornered slow moving vehicle sign, visible in this illustration, has caused much concern and consternation for all Amish people. Many have served jail sentences over the past 30 years for refusing to affix the gaudy orange insignia to the backs of their buggies. The last such incident resulted in an Amish man spending three days in jail in Carrolltown, Pennsylvania for refusing to pay a small fine. To have paid the fine would have been to agree that he was "guilty in the eyes of the Lord." They feel that the bright colored insignia will draw attention to man and away from God. And, since the sign is also required on tractors and other "worldly" machinery, many refuse to use it fearing they will be in conflict with the Biblical dictate, "Be ye not unequally yoked with non-believers."

The Slow Moving Vehicle Sign Controversy

The Old Order Amish are finding it more and more difficult not to be "modern man" in the 21st Century. As noted above, impingement and persecution come from several different sources. Local, state and national legislators often pass new laws without the consent, knowledge or consideration of different minority groups. As noted, a case in point is a law in existence in several states requiring a triangular-shaped, reflective emblem to be affixed to the back of all slow-moving vehicles (the SMV).

The Amish, in most states, view this three-cornered gaudy orange emblem as a hex symbol, or *"the mark of the beast"* as described in the *Bible* and have refused to affix it to their buggies. They do not believe that they should use this type of taboo orange emblem as a symbol for their protection. They further believe that the colorful emblem would glorify man rather than God. In several communities the Amish offered to use neutral colored reflector tape in an attempt at compromise. This compromise has been granted in several locations but it has failed in others and the Amish men there (I am only aware of one female being placed in jail for this offense) were forced to serve short jail terms.

As noted, many times compromises are reached. But such compromises are tentative and can change overnight with a political change in state or county government. This SMV controversy began almost 30 years ago and, in some localities, remains a problem even in the new millennium. For example, in December 2000 an Amish man chose to spend three days in jail rather than pay a small fine for not putting the SMV triangle on his buggy as required by state law in Pennsylvania. The young Amish male, age 22, made it clear that he thought the insignia violated the religious beliefs of his Amish faith.

Although this incident was/is extremely serious to the Amish, *Time Magazine* (December 18, 2000) poked fun at the Amish man involved in this controversy in a brief write-up of this unfortunate incident. *Time* explained the plight of the jailed Amish man as follows:

"News Quiz: An Amish man jailed for not putting an orange warning sticker on his buggy was allowed to: a) Whittle a shiv out of lye soap? b) Wear his own dark clothes instead of the prison's orange ones? or c) Churn coke with Robert Downey Jr.?"

The answer was "b" as he was permitted to wear his Amish clothes while spending the three days in jail (*Time*, December 18, 2000). I fail to see the humor in this obviously very stressful, religious freedom issue. And, I'm certain, if they were to read *Time* (of course they will not), neither would the Old Order Amish. There are several documented cases of Amish men serving their jail time wearing only their long underwear to avoid wearing the "worldly" clothing.

An additional ten Amish men were arrested in the same Pennsylvania community mentioned above for replacing the three cornered, orange colored, insignia on the backs of their buggies with the less offensive, gray reflective tape. The presiding judge fined each man $100 and/or ordered each to do community service. The Amish men in question did not pay their fines nor carry out the community service as to do so would have implied "guilt in the eyes of the Lord."

I was present several years ago when a test was conducted to determine the effectiveness of using either reflective tape or the required slow moving vehicle sign on the back of a buggy as a warning to approaching motorists. We conducted the test at night using a car with its lights on, slowly backing up into the darkness behind the two buggies. It was obvious to all present that the reflective tape being used in that specific Amish community was clearly superior to the SMV sign. However, a local judge there refused to grant the use of the tape as a substitute and clearly let it be known of his intent to enforce the law.

It is obvious that this controversy is far from over as only four states currently permit the Amish to use reflective tape on the back of their buggies as a substitute for the orange triangle sign the Amish find so offensive.

New Amish Home-Based Enterprises

As noted above, the long held practice of farming has enabled the Amish to live a life distinctly separate from the larger secular society surrounding them. However, this has changed rather dramatically in the past two decades. One of the best examples of this is Lancaster County Pennsylvania, the first American home for the Amish. Prices for farmland in Lancaster have doubled, or quadrupled, over the past 15 or so years.

The Amish simply cannot afford such prices. If the entire, immediate family is willing to relocate, then migration often occurs. It is not at all uncommon for 10-15 Amish families to pick up and move from an established Amish settlement such as Lancaster County to a new area of the US or Mexico in search of less expensive farmland. Their *Bible* clearly tells them that, if maintaining their way of life is no longer possible, or if things aren't going well where they are and their *"wells are being stopped up,"* they *"should move to new lands."*

However, for many Amish families, migrating to find available land for farming would undermine their family-centered tradition. Thus, as mentioned above, they are quickly, and successfully, shifting to other ways of making a living. As noted, many have gone to work in non-union factories and related industries. However, the Amish have recently discovered home based cottage industries and businesses in a big way.

Many of these new, entirely rural enterprises have grown quite large and, in turn, employ not only the entire family, but other Amish as well. This change has resulted in some important challenges to the Amish ways of church and family life. However, in my opinion, home businesses do not adversely affect the highly prized, Amish value of having the whole family working together as a unit in one location, preferably, the home. Many Amish who have now gone into these home based businesses had been working away from home in factories and negative, unwanted changes for their respective families resulted. That is, only one parent was at home during the day, etc. For these families, factory work was not in keeping with the long held Amish standard of being "family centered" and, according to many Amish ministers, was/is, undermining their way of life.

The Amish in Lancaster County, Pennsylvania best illustrate this shift in the Amish methods of livelihood to small business ventures. Data indicate that some twenty years ago only around 5% of the Amish in Lancaster County worked in non-farm businesses. Now, in 2005, that number is more like 50% and growing. This is a consequential shift for the Amish population and many experts have predicted that it will bring about long term, negative affects to their way of life. However, I do not believe that this shift will turn the Amish away from their long held traditions. In actuality, the type home businesses they are initiating will help to maintain, enhance and even strengthen their way of life. That is, having small businesses at their homes will keep them close to their families, neighbors and others in the community. This has always been the family rearing practice of choice for the Amish.

However, home based businesses are fraught with potential pitfalls for the Amish and their way of life. For example, those who have begun enterprises at home have had to learn to deal appropriately with employee and government regulations, etc. And of course, with the English as a sought after consumer, there is more exposure to the non-Amish with their worldly views and actions. This over exposure to non-Amish people concerns the Amish greatly, especially where their children are involved.

The venture into personal, home-related businesses raises some other troubling questions for the Amish church and its leaders. I was asked recently by a sociologist if this occupational shift means that Amish women will now begin their own business ventures thereby affecting the size of families and the overall, traditional male/female relationship structure within the Amish communities. If this did occur, it would undermine the Amish faith in such a manner so as to threaten the sect's very existence. Several Amish elders have made it clear to me that they will not permit this to happen to their group. I do believe that Amish women, as they have done for years, will continue to sew quilts for sale to the non-Amish buyers, will continue their road side sale of fruits and vegetables to tourists and others, etc. Many Amish women are also working as cooks and waiters in tourist restaurants advertised as serving "real Amish food." However, I am convinced that Amish women will not enter into any cottage businesses alone, but only as they work alongside their husbands and children.

A cultural anthropology friend recently asked me if the Amish communities would now splinter into class structures as these small, home based businesses prosper. Personally, I also do not believe that this will occur. Matter of fact, to counter this possibility, most Old Order Amish churches have restricted the size of these small home-based businesses. That is, the number of those employed by one particular Amish enterprise is restricted to a small number of individuals and the church encourages employing only immediate family members where possible. One Amish church community with which I am familiar, has restricted each such family enterprise to only three or four outside the immediate family employees and all must be Amish employees.

In addition, the Amish have had to accommodate themselves to tourists in ways that they could formerly avoid. Businesses need customers to succeed, and tourists compose the largest number of customers for many Amish businesses in the new millennium. As noted above, this has brought about a great increase and alteration in the interaction between Amish and non-Amish people. To say the least, Amish leaders are deeply concerned that their way of life could be altered greatly by the increase in relationships with their non-Amish customers.

Some Amish have also ventured into uniquely different occupations than would ever have been sanctioned by the church just a few years ago. Joseph, a 12-year-old Amish boy writes about one such Amish man and his "new" occupation.

A Used Horse Salesman

My dad says that _____ is a really good horseman. He really knows a good horse when he sees one and makes a part of his living at the English harness race tracks. He does not go there as a gambler and does not go to watch the horse races. He is a used horse salesman. He buys old race horses from race horse trainers and sells them to other Amish as buggy horses. Dad says that since these horses have already been trained to pull race carts, they are already well trained to pull buggies. The English horse owners sometimes give him the worn out racers as that is better than having to feed them or having to send them to the glue factory. I think this is a good thing for _____ to do.

Joseph, eighth grade

As noted, I for one believe that this new Amish enterprise system will actually contribute positively to their way of life. Such enterprises will keep the family together, especially the young, and will help to preserve Amish traditions. In addition, setting up a young married couple in a small business venture is much less expensive than helping them to purchase a farm with today's prices. To me as a former Amish sect member, the most important aspect regarding these small, home based cottage industries is that the Amish customs of hard work and frugality continue to serve them very well as they increasingly integrate into a capitalistic society. In addition, they have worked diligently down through the years so as to not jeopardize the integrity of their long held family-centered traditions and have been very successful at doing so. This is a remarkable feat and highly commendable. And, the Amish will continue to be successful at maintaining and enhancing this time honored tradition, even without farming as their sole source of income.

The Amish are proving to be excellent entrepreneurs and their businesses are growing in leaps and bounds. According to a 2004 directory of Amish businesses, there were over 2500 such enterprises in and around Lancaster County, Pennsylvania. The same thing is occurring wherever Old Order Amish are located. And, the Amish customs of hard work and frugality serve them well in these endeavors as their small business ventures seldom fail.

One basic reason for this success of their small businesses is the fact that practically all of the machinery they use in their home based businesses is obsolete in the non-Amish market and can be purchased from non-Amish at bargain prices. This, of course, is in keeping with their creed to "be different from the world." The Amish are very skilled at taking this obsolete machinery and remodeling it to accommodate their non-use of electronics. I recently visited an Amish buggy and carriage making business in Indiana and was amazed at the ancient age of some of these excellent working machines I saw there. Many would be considered antiques by non-Amish standards.

Another reason for their success in the small business arena is the fact, as noted above, that Congress has exempted the Amish from social-security taxes and that they are not required to pay into the workers' compensation fund. Thus, there are no health-related expenses and no retirement benefits to pay for Amish employees. This fact upsets some local non-Amish businesses that compete with the Amish for customers. Of course, if the Amish business has non-Amish employees, all such benefits would have to be paid for each of them. Thus, one seldom finds non-Amish employees working in Amish businesses. This fact also upsets some local non-Amish who have accused the Amish businessmen of discrimination in their hiring practices.

I am of the opinion that the Amish ministers and bishops saw this move away from farming coming years ago but were reluctant to discuss it. The switch has now occurred and the Amish leaders and elders are wondering aloud how this will eventually affect the Amish family. Several Amish leaders have told me of their fear that the values, their principles, their standards and their rules for living they cherish, will be adversely affected. What will actually happen is not completely clear at this time in their history. No doubt it was much simpler and easier to sustain their simplistic way of life while living as a farm family. However, the Amish are a tenacious people and I'm betting that their way of life will continue in spite of these rather dramatic changes in their methods of making their daily living as small business owners.

Problems with Social Security

In general, Americans may feel that Social Security is a good idea. However, it has, in the past, caused immeasurable problems for the Amish who view it as a form of insurance (which is strictly taboo). Many an Amish farmer lost good cattle and horses confiscated by the Internal Revenue Service men during the middle sixties for failure to pay Social Security even though they would never collect a dime of it! There are many documented stories told about this problem. When the IRS men came to an Amish farm to confiscate livestock, the non-aggressive Amish would unselfishly assist them in choosing the livestock they felt would best make up for their lack of paying Social Security. They were always kind to the IRS men and many local newspapers carried stories about these men being taken into the house, given coffee, fed and in one case they loaded the livestock and then went fishing with the Amishman in his farm pond. Other stores reveal how the government men often left with the confiscated livestock with tears in their eyes. However, unlike many other controversies involving the Amish, this one has a happy ending. A rider was attached to the Medicare Bill exempting all Amish people from paying Social Security.

Paved Roads

Local governments often build paved roads through Amish communities which bring fast cars and camera-toting tourists to the Amish farmlands. These roads also play havoc to horses' feet. A horse simply cannot be continually driven on concrete, but local governments have not seen fit to leave grassy strips on either side of the new roads to drive on, explaining the cost as being prohibitive. Also, the Old Order Amish come under continual harassment as they drive along these roads in their open buggies. It is especially popular to harass the young Amish men and their girlfriends as they travel along in their open horse-drawn buggies. Several adults and children have been seriously injured, in more than one case fatally, as the horse bolted after being frightened by passing motorists. One of the most publicized deaths was that of a sleeping infant killed instantly by a piece of asphalt thrown from a passing car. The child was asleep in the rear of the buggy and the parents, unaware that the child had been hit, discovered the death upon reaching their home more than an hour later!

This tragic incident resulted in the movie, *A Stoning in Fulham County*. The movie depicts how harassing the buggy driving Amish in Fulham County (fictitious) was/is almost a rite of passage into manhood for teenage males. However, on this particular night, the practice resulted in tragedy. It was obvious from the story line that the harassing of the Amish in this particular part of the country had been going on for many years. Several adult men, including the county sheriff, in a pitiful attempt at defending the young men indicates: "I harassed the Amish when I was young, we all did."

Non-Amish youth frequently invade the Amish communities at night and perform such harassments as turning out livestock, upsetting outdoor toilets and burning corn and wheat shocks. This is especially prevalent during Halloween or when America is at war. These same culprits, realizing that the defenseless Amishman's religion prevents his calling the local sheriff, will pull a buggy behind a car or truck at high speed and release it to crash into bits and pieces against the road bank or tree.

Some Additional
Twenty-First Century Problems

Outdated Child Labor Laws

In 1997 a US Labor Department official cited 1938 child labor laws as a reason to interrogate a half-dozen underage Amish boys regarding their sawmill apprentice jobs in a small, Pennsylvania, Old Order Amish community. Following the questioning, the labor official sent the boys home and threatened that if they returned to work, the government would confiscate every board, machine and building at the Amish owned sawmill. The interpretation prevented Amish business owners from even allowing Amish youth to sweep sawdust, stack wood, or operate a cash register on the premises where woodworking tools were being used. Stiff fines upwards of $20,000 were imposed on the Amish owners.

Amish youth graduate from textbooks, after 8 years of formal schooling, to a hands-on vocational education program at age 14-15. The successful apprenticeship program emphasizes such practical skills as farming, carpentry, and home-making. Due in part to this program, Amish families rarely experience the problems of teenage violence, drugs, or single motherhood afflicting our larger society. Working as an apprentice with an older, skilled Amish craftsman is structured to maintain and enhance their culture.

The weekly Amish newspaper, *The Budget*, carried the sawmill story and Amish across the US were profoundly shocked and had difficulty understanding the reasons for the government's intrusion into the apprenticeship program. The Amish viewed the Labor Department's action as an encroachment on a religious based program that embraced proven, old-fashioned, self-sufficient and unique child rearing techniques. In essence, the interpretation interfered with a long held tradition of the rearing of youngsters under the supervision of model, older members of the Amish church who are themselves expert craftsmen. These selected Amish mentors only intent was to assist the youth of their culture in learning a specific trade while simultaneously serving as a model of "Amishness" for their young charges. The government officials were claiming to protect the Amish minors. However, in my opinion, they were doing the opposite! This unfortunate episode is an example of the concept of "assumed similarity" at its worse!

Advocates for the Amish argued that during shop classes public school students use all sorts of power tools, including table saws, to make projects. Often there is only one adult supervisor for a class of 25 or 30. But we don't talk about ending shop classes or fining schools that offer such classes. In 1972 the Supreme Court ruled that the Amish have the right to terminate their children's formal education at the eighth grade level. Typically, these "graduated" youth work on farms (minors working in agriculture are exempt from child labor laws), but as the availability of land decreases in the Amish communities, these Amish youth have moved on to apprenticeships in woodworking shops, sawmills and other home based enterprises. The US Department of Labor's 1997 interpretation of the child labor laws kept any Amish youth under the age of 18 from legally working in these shops and, in essence, had shut down the Amish vocational educational program.

In my opinion, the Labor Department's action was about one segment of our society using force to impose its majority views on a religious minority. The government officials failed to understand that this apprenticeship program is part of the Amish plan of education and accordingly, should not be a crime in our freedom loving country. Fortunately, a Congressman from Pennsylvania agreed and took positive action to rectify the problem.

New Labor Law Affords Amish Exemptions

In 1998, Congressman Joseph Pitts (R-PA) introduced legislation to amend the 1938 Labor Standards Act. Pitts introduced the legislation three times before it was signed into law by President Bush in 2005. The amendment, introduced into the Senate by Arlen Specter (R-PA), states that child labor is not oppressive to an individual who works in or outside a business where machinery is used to process wood, if that person is at least 14, but under the age of 18, and is a member of a religious sect or division whose teachings do not permit formal education beyond the eighth grade. Employment is permitted if the youth is supervised by an adult relative or member of the same religious sect. As Congressman Pitts stated, *"The enactment of the Amish Labor law allows the Amish to continue the way of life they have enjoyed since their arrival here in America. As they are allowed to live in freedom, so shall we."*

Genetic Problems

Past inbreeding among the Amish, as mentioned previously, is currently a very serious problem and appears to be getting worse as many second cousin marriages continue. In the following article an Amish writer succinctly, and in a scholarly manner, details the problem. He also chastises Amish leaders for not doing more about the problem.

———————●———————

The Laws of Heredity

...In the last twenty years there has been an alarming increase in genetic weaknesses and diseases among the plain communities. Some of these are cystic fibrosis, hemophilia, dwarfism, muscular dystrophy, albinoism and Maple Syrup Urine Disease.

But why should the Amish and Mennonites have more such inherited problems than other people? Is it a special judgment of God upon us? Is it a sign that we are weaker than other people?

No, it is none of these. It is simply the laws of heredity going into effect. It is due to our limited gene pool. Because we tend to marry within our own communities for generations, we become more closely related to each other than the general population. Even those of us who think we are not related to each other often find that if we trace back our family lines, we share a common ancestor or two.

...What can be done about it?

Surely the first step is to become aware of the problem. I am often appalled by our lack of even being aware that there is a problem. In one community, where marrying is permitted between first cousins and severe hereditary problems are showing up, a member of the community said, when asked about first-cousin marriages—"Well, I guess it is still better than going out into the world to marry."

In another instance, in a community where in some cases nearly the entire family is confined to wheelchairs, a bishop was heard to remark resignedly, "Well, I always feel that God is sending us these cases to see if we are willing to take care of them."

It certainly is a commendable attitude not to want to marry people who do not share our faith, as it is commendable to care for the crippled and needy. But there is nothing Christian about ignoring the laws of nature that God has fixed and put into place when He created an orderly world. The laws of heredity are a part of that creation, and if we ignore them it is to our own hurt. The best gift we can bestow upon future generations is to make every intelligent effort within our power and ability to ensure that they do not inherit genetic weaknesses from us.

...And once we have faced the problem, and become aware that it is a problem, we need to search for some solutions. Since the problem is the result of inbreeding over too many generations, a giant step in the right direction would be to widen the genetic scope of our young people's potential partners. This is especially urgent in those communities where the young people almost never marry outside the home community, and into which no new families move from other communities. This means that generation after generation the young people marry into the same families, with no new genes entering the community. Given enough time, this is almost a sure formula to genetic disaster, and once problems become visible, we have waited plenty long to seek solutions. Church leaders and parents need to recognize that it is important for a community to have genetic diversity. This can be brought about by more interaction between communities in the form of visiting or moving. Welcoming converts from outside our plain circles will also greatly help this problem, though that in itself would be a questionable motive for encouraging converts!

Another step we might take would be to discourage seeking partners who are too closely related. I personally feel it is high time to take another step, and work toward the elimination of second cousin marriages, also.

Yes, I know our forefathers always married second cousins. Which is exactly the reason it may no longer be wise for us to do so!

Another solution that should become apparent to us is to discourage those who have serious genetic weaknesses from marrying, at least during their child-bearing years. For when even one partner has the actual weakness, it will be inherited by a given percentage of his or her children. Perhaps I should state this again to make it clearer. When only the gene is defective, both partners need to have the same gene defective, before the disease shows up in the children. If however, a person has the actual defect itself, and gets married, he or she will pass it on to a given percentage of the children. That is why it would seem an act of mercy and prudence for such a person to voluntarily forego the right to marry....

E.S., *Family Life*

Another Amishman, responding to the above essay in *Family Life*, writes about how his intermarriage (**"our grandparents were related on both sides, our parents were related on both sides, and we were related on both sides"**) caused the birth of two retarded children in his family.

Two Retarded Children

...Do not get me wrong—we take the very best care to provide so that our two retarded children can have it as nice as possible. The one can barely walk any more, and the other one has had several surgeries, in an attempt to improve his walking, but to no avail.

When our first one was born and as soon as it was noticed that the baby was retarded, we got so much advice as to where to go and how this or that person got help. They meant it well. We went to different doctors and also one of the most noted clinics in the United States, all to no avail. It is just as the article stated, if the genes are in both parents, it is like planting corn and hoping to harvest oats. When we married, we were just as unconcerned about genes as I think most other young couples in love are. We did not give a thought that our grandparents were related on both sides, our parents were related on both sides, and we were related on both sides.

In our area there are several family lines especially high in degenerative factors such as mental retardation and "Smallism." Perhaps most people do not realize that a high percent of the dwarfs in the United States are Amish, without a doubt due to inbreeding.

We have in our area several large families where the parents are second cousins. Some of the children are quite short and have other distinctive features. In our particular church area most of the people are related to each other, if you trace back four or five generations.

Some people say, in an unconcerned manner, that in Biblical times the old patriarchs married close relatives without any apparent adverse effects. Please do not use this excuse in our day or you may be sorry later.

Anonymous—Reprinted from *Family Life*

Most Amish are aware of this very serious problem. However, since the Amish are so inter-related, tend to stay close to home, seldom travel and continue to shun marrying outside the church, it is my opinion that this sect-threatening problem will only get worse before it gets better.

The Problems with Tourists

One of the Amish counties being most threatened by urbanization and progress as we enter the new millennium Lancaster County, Pennsylvania—the Amish heartland. Civilization is refusing to go along with the Amish in Lancaster and some Amish are leaving it. This is the county first offered as a sanctuary to the Amish by William Penn when he toured Europe.

The Amish in this beautiful area of Pennsylvania are the target of several thousand tourists per year. Tourists travel through the county's back roads in tour buses or sometimes rent buggies and are often a nuisance to the Amish. The Amish write about their tourist problems to the *Budget* and *Family Life* telling of the rudeness of tourists. Recently, an Amish scribe wrote to the *Budget* describing how a busload of tourists trampled his garden in pursuit of a picture of his family as they worked in the garden. In all fairness, most tourists are respectful of the Amish. It is those ignorant of the Amish values and ways who cause the Amish problems.

Traveling through Lancaster County one finds an endless string of "Amish" motels, "Amish" food, "Amish" restaurants, "Amish" gift shops, "Amish" museums, "Amish" amusement parks and so forth. Tourism in this one Amish community is now a multi-million dollar a year business!

In the winter time, one can travel though Lancaster County going through such tiny Amish villages as Paradise, Intercourse, and Blueballs, which have been left undisturbed for over a 100 years. There one sees the horse and buggy driving Amish, water wheels, windmills and other sights reminiscent of 200 years ago. But, in the summer time the mood changes to a carnival atmosphere as bumper to bumper traffic and billboards indicate that "it's real—it's genuine, you're here. Visit the house and farm occupied by the German-speaking Amish, stop and talk to these genuine Amish people." A tourist's inquisitiveness can quickly become a nuisance to the Amish who strive to avoid publicity and photographs at all costs.

As the following essay indicates, tourists are also often **"disrespectful"** and even **"rude."** I urge anyone who plans to tour an Amish community to please read the following very carefully. Also, take care to learn about the uniqueness of some of the Amish values and ways prior to your visit.

How I Tried to Get Rid of the Rude

It was a pleasant morning in July. A refreshing rain the night before had put the soil into a nice condition to cultivate. We live beside a state highway and I was working steadily and paying little attention to the usual flow of traffic. I had my mind on my work for as soon as I was finished, I would have some other things to do.

I heard a car slow down and stop in front of me. When I looked up from my work, the woman in the car had her camera turned on me and at that instant it clicked. She waved her hand and drove on.

I was disgusted but when I thought of the picture which the woman had gotten, it almost amused me. A plump, barefooted woman, red in the face from the heat, with an old, not-too-clean dress on, pushing a hand cultivator. But the vegetable and flower plants looked nice so maybe her picture wasn't too bad after all . This woman hadn't asked permission, she simply took the picture and went on.

I wished she would have asked permission, but I've learned that even though some ask, they don't intend to respect your wishes. For example, last summer I went to a shopping center with my daughter-in-law. She went in first and when I came in, she warned me, "There's a lady in here who says she's from Switzerland and she's taking all the pictures she can get. When she asked me to take mine, I said no, but she just watched her chance and took it anyhow."

The lady was standing by the entry doors which faces the hitching racks and was taking pictures of people putting their groceries on the buggies. This woman asked permission but when it wasn't granted, she took them anyhow. In a way, this seemed even ruder than not asking in the first place.

But the most unpleasant experience I ever had with photo hunters was several years ago. The reason it was so unpleasant was because this time it was not just the tourist that was rude. I had my horse hitched to the surrey and had 4 or 5 of the children with me and was going to my sister's house. My nerves were tense as I turned north for I always dreaded this one mile on a U.S. highway. "Well," I tried to console myself, "surely the factory workers have all gone to work already so there shouldn't be so much traffic on the highway now."

It wasn't too bad and we had gone about half the distance when a car passed me. "Tourists," I said when I saw how they looked back and watched us. Then they turned around and approached us slowly from the rear and I saw they had a camera ready. "Put your heads down," I told the children on the front seat and I also put mine down.

They stopped beside the road in front of us and we passed them and I urged my horse on. I watched for the car to pass us again but they stayed behind us until the highway was clear from both ways. Suddenly the horse jumped and I saw they were passing us on the wrong side. When they were in front of us they suddenly pulled across the road in front of us. I pulled the lines up tight hoping none of the children would slide off the seat because of my sudden stop.

Suddenly I realized they had us where they wanted us. I couldn't put my head down because I had to control my horse and the children were too curious to see what was going on. I felt anger rising up inside me and before I knew what was happening I was yelling at them, "The nerve of some people!" I don't know if I shook my fist or not but at least I almost felt like it.

Of course just at that moment the camera clicked and I could see they greatly enjoyed my annoyance. Right away I felt ashamed of myself. I checked both ways for traffic and drove past without looking at them. They soon went around us again and this time they were laughing and waving their hands mockingly as they sped away.

Just then we turned off the highway and went our way. At first, I felt upset but after I had time to think, I was thoroughly ashamed of myself. What kind of a witness had I been to these people? Would it make them respect the Amish any more? And what did God think of me? Just because they were rude didn't make it right for me to be the same. Maybe their actions didn't look worse to Him under the circumstances than mine did.

When they were crucifying Jesus, causing Him almost unbearable pain, He prayed for them, "Father, forgive them, for they know not what they do." But here I couldn't even take a little mocking and rudeness from these people without getting angry. Maybe God lets things like this happen to try us out. And I have also found out that not all tourists are rude and disrespectful.

Several years ago one evening my husband and I were at the sale of a friend of ours in town. We left our horse at the hitching rack beside the blacksmith shop. I stood beside the buggy and my husband was tying the horse when a car drove in beside us. A man and a woman came out and the woman asked, "Would you mind if we took your pictures standing beside your rig?"

"We'd rather not," answered my husband.

"Thank you," said the lady. "We just didn't know."

We looked the other way and started walking toward the alley. My husband said to me, "They'll probably get us anyway."

I couldn't resist a glance backward and was surprised to see them walking away. They had respected our wishes and didn't take any pictures.

When we happen to have wheat or oats in a field alongside the road, people are always interested in seeing us cut it. The sight of a binder being pulled by four horses, and with someone shocking the grain has stopped many a car. Some only watch but others take pictures. If the threshing machine is operating close to the road, the same thing happens, and they ask to take pictures. These people have never been taught anything different and they use their cameras, somewhat like we use our diary. Where should we draw the line?

Human nature being what it is, I suppose we will always have the politely interested, the curious and the rude people. But I hope, with the help of God, I will never again lose my temper when I meet up with the latter kind.

Anonymous—Reprinted from *Family Life*

———————●—————

Tourism in Lancaster began only 40 or so years ago, but is now a bonanza for the owners. They succeeded well beyond their wildest dreams and today Pennsylvania Dutch country is one of the largest tourist attractions in the United States. As many as 20,000 visitors a day in season swarm down over the Amish back roads. As the above essay verifies, they snap pictures of the Amish whose *Bible* admonishes them not to have "a graven image"—a picture made of themselves. This is also the reason behind the "face-less" Amish dolls. Tourists often do not ask permission to take pictures. They snap pictures from their car windows and some have burst uninvited into the easily accessible, quaint, inviting Old Order Amish school houses. The following are short excerpts from letters written (from Amish teachers) to the editors of *Blackboard Bulletin*, the Amish educational journal, about their problems with tourists.

———————●—————

Tourists at School

...Most times tourists seem a nuisance to me, but I guess if I were traveling for pleasure, I would like to travel slowly and ask a lot of questions, too. I do not like it when they take pictures of the children, and I often ask or motion for them to move on. Some do but others are determined to have a picture. I try not to allow the children to call out "no pictures" or to make faces, nor are they to run out to the fence when a car stops. But it seems that it is hard for the little ones just to keep on playing....

———→●←———

...My opinion about tourists in school is the less we have the better off we are. I also feel if we would give them a start there would be no end to it.

———→●←———

...Why do I object to tourists stopping at school? First, it is a distraction to pupils who are supposed to be studying, especially if they come up to the windows and peep in. Some are even bold enough to open the door without knocking. Some are polite enough to knock and ask for admittance, but are so hideously dressed you feel embarrassed at the expression on the pupils' faces when they come in. If they are allowed to come in, they don't seem interested in the school more than for curiosity's sake. I just feel better without them around....

Anonymous—All reprinted from *Blackboard Bulletin*

———→●←———

During a trip back to my former Amish community, I experienced the true affects of "Amish Tourism" first hand. I was attending an Amish farm auction, that of a late uncle, when the serenity of the peaceful, horse and buggy environment was suddenly broken by the loud noise of two large Greyhound buses. The dust created by the buses on the non-paved road was tremendous. Both buses came to a stop directly in front of the huge, mainly Amish, auction crowd. All present knew that behind those non-see-through tinted bus windows were many cameras with powerful zoom lenses. Many turned their backs. An Amish cousin, standing next to me, summed up his and my feelings succinctly when he whispered, "It's like we're in a zoo, isn't it?"

Tourism is of marginal benefit to the Amish by their own choice. They are not in the entertainment, nor the hotel and motel business. However, many do erect roadside stands from which they sell quilts, vegetables, and so forth, to the tourists. One of the most damaging aspects of the tourism is that Lancaster County and other Amish settlements have now been "discovered" and the Amish farmers can no more buy more land than they can buy gold. People who are benefiting the most from the Amish leaving the farms are local industry owners. Amish men and women have been groomed to awaken early in the morning and work is a moral directive. Those now working in non-governmental factories and so forth no longer have to get up so early. And, they make excellent factory workers, but as previously mentioned, often unhappy ones.

Feeding the Tourists

As noted elsewhere, most Old Order Amish want to be left alone to live their lives as they see fit. However, the tourists have arrived in the Amish communities and are increasing in number every summer.

I believe tourism has flourished among the Amish because non-Amish thought that the quaint sect they saw in the movie *Witness*, documentaries and magazine articles, would soon disappear from the American scene. In addition, many non-Amish truly have an appreciation for the way the Amish live and have the desire to (someday, just maybe) emulate their practically stress-free way of living. Thus, they become tourists in the Amish areas because they simply want to "see" for themselves if it really is possible to live in the manner in which the Amish are living today. And, I've had tourists tell me that they secretly hope, by visiting the slow-paced Amish, that just maybe they will learn something that will help them to slow down the stressful and frenetic world they find themselves living in on a daily basis.

Many Amish are finding tourists as fascinating as they are irritating. That is, tourists have become a confusing abomination. However, some are also finding them very profitable. For example, some Amish housewives are taking in small groups of non-Amish tourists for dinner, the noontime meal (Amish do not use the word "lunch"), and then for brief discussions and singing, etc. afterward. Of course, it is expected that a "donation" of a certain amount per person will be given. Recently, an Amish family in a Midwestern state was ordered to stop this practice, by county officials, unless they purchased a restaurant license. Of course, such a purchase would be out of the question for many reasons. However, most importantly, the Amish church would never permit such a license since the Amish home is where church services are held and is thus considered a religious "sanctuary."

Recently, a retired Amish male was ordered to stop giving buggy rides and tours of blacksmith shops, etc. to tourists (again, for donations and tips) unless he obtained a special license and liability insurance. Of course, he had no choice but to stop the practice. Many other such incidents could be given here.

Vacationing in Florida

For several years now, many Amish adults have been traveling to Florida (they employ an outsider driver or ride a bus) for "medicinal" purposes. However, it is common knowledge that most are simply taking winter vacations in Florida. So as not to excessively clash with their religious principles, they do so exclusively in Pinecraft, a Florida Gulf Coast town near Sarasota. Many second homes of Amish are clustered there and one often finds two or three Amish families, mostly older adults, staying in the same home. And, more and more advertisements offering homes for sale, or rent, in Pinecraft are appearing in the *Budget*. Of course, the Amish do not bring their horses and buggies with them to Pinecraft and, in adhering to the Biblical principles to be *"different and to not conform to the world,"* the quaintly dressed Amish can be seen on the quiet streets of Pinecraft riding adult size, three-wheeled tricycles!

Even though ministers continue to urge against such practices as Florida vacations, such changes are probably inevitable. I have visited this Florida Amish community on several occasions and have seen the numbers of these "temporary" residents increase in the past decade. This past winter it was estimated that some 1500 Amish made the trip to Florida. However, again, I do not believe that this will jeopardize the Amish way of life, or their rules for living, to any noticeable extent.

The Issue of Using "Worldly" Things

Non-Amish individuals will often ask me about the obvious conflict the Amish face on a daily basis when it comes to *"living in the world but not being a part of the world."* Obviously, there are many such conflicts and several examples could be cited here.

One such example concerns something we in the modern world take for granted; our personal grooming. That is, for example, whether to use home remedies or store purchased products for our personal grooming is not something we worry about. And, although it may seem trite to the reader, this is of major concern to the Amish who attempt to *"remain apart from the world"* in all they do. For example, an Amish monthly magazine, Young Companion, recently featured a four-page spread concerning the use of store purchased deodorants and perfumes and whether Amish should or should not use them. The feature was titled **"Can you Help Me?"** and begins with a reader asking: **"Is smelling 'sour' actually better than using deodorant or perfume?"**

In essence, the writer is wondering aloud which would be worse for an Amish person; to have bad odor or to use the taboo *"worldly"* perfumes and deodorants? The published responses received from other Amish individuals demonstrates the turmoil and inner conflict the Amish often face in the modern world when it comes to even the simplest aspects of life. That is, with their over developed conscience, this reveals how much they anguish over the issue of using *"worldly"* products in their every day lives; products and conveniences that we, *"worldly"* people, take for granted.

One respondent to the feature, an Amish minister, wrote about this conflict and answered the above question in this manner: **"As a Christian, it should be our desire to not be offensive. Neither should we follow worldliness. A proper, non-perfumed deodorant may be helpful in some cases, although nothing is better than just plain smelling clean."** Concerning the use of perfume he states: **"Using an artificial scent to attract attention is more in line with worldly attire than Christian simplicity. When I see a dresser with a dozen different scents displayed, I get the impression of vanity. Think it over."**

Another writes: **"Being clean is commendable. Perhaps washing or bathing more often would help."** Basically, this writer believes that using a non-smelling store bought deodorant may be ok and within the rules of the church. But, concerning perfume, he states: **"A sincere Christian girl is ashamed to 'advertise' herself in this way and should never ever use perfume."**

Another Amish respondent is opposed to using either deodorant or perfume and writes: **"God would have us take care of our bodies by washing and bathing regularly. We should strive to leave no offensive body odors."** He further states that he is opposed to perfumes and deodorants because they are **"Used to attract attention. I cannot believe this is God's will."**

Another writes about the reactions perfume scents cause and states: **"A Christian young lady should not smell the same as the harlot on the streets. Think about the** names **of worldly perfumes. What thoughts do they bring up? I consider perfume to be a cosmetic to be avoided by Christians."**

Another reader of the monthly Amish magazine writes as follows: **"I would feel safe to say that the majority of people who use nationally advertised scents and perfumes do so for two reasons—because they are dissatisfied with the way they were created, or they wish to draw attention to themselves."**

One writer feels strongly that the Amish should not use perfumes as they are designed and manufactured for only one reason: **."..to entice and arouse those of the opposite sex."**

Several respondents to the question posed above gave suggestions for other products to use instead of regular store bought deodorants used by worldly people: **"For the last 10 years I have been using Le Crystal, also known as 'The Rock.' It is compressed salt and neutralizes the sweat as you perspire and prevents objectionable odors. It doesn't stain clothes or clog pores yet allows me to perspire as the Creator intended."**

Another suggested using a product known as "Lavilin." and explained: **"It is a natural product made from a certain flower and works by killing the bacteria that cause the odor."**

Several also suggested that the questioner use baking soda. One wrote: **"Put a teaspoon of baking soda in the palm of your hand, sprinkle a little water on it to make a paste and then rub it under your arms. Rinse, and if necessary repeat the procedure until you smell clean."**

There are many aspects of life that we in the modern world deem as simple, everyday situations and we may have difficulty understanding the consternation shown by the Amish to this situation as described. However, as demonstrated throughout this book, there are many aspects of everyday living that we in the modern world don't even give a second thought that cause great and sincere anguish among the Amish.

Many such aspects of every day life could be described here. The point being, although is it becoming more and more difficult not to be a modern and *"worldly"* person, the Amish will keep working at being *"different"* and *"non-worldly"* in all they do. They do not view this as a task or as a chore, it is simply following God's way on this earth so that they will, one day, go to a better place.

Some Perplexing Compromises With Progress

As indicated throughout this book, the horse and buggy Amish have resisted many of the more modern aspects of the progressive world surrounding them. Yet, although they have basically stood still over the years, they have flourished and have seen their culture grow in unprecedented numbers. Most authors writing about the Amish are convinced that they have accomplished this feat by producing large families (approximately 7 children per family with 85% of them remaining Amish for life) and by resisting America's melting pot concept of cultural assimilation. However, I am of the opinion that the major reason for the Amish culture's ability to thrive while maintaining and enhancing their slow-paced, stress free lifestyle, has been their willingness to make small, but significant, compromises with the spirit of progress.

It is an undeniable fact that the Amish are slowly changing, but only to a carefully thought out, measured extent. They are reluctant to change at all and do so only when such change does not *jeopardize the integrity of the basic tenets of their religion or conflict with their values and moral code.* That is, they will not compromise nor negotiate with "worldly" progress if it disrupts family and/or community stability or if it appears that it may in any way negatively impinge on the future of their way of life. In addition, there is a strong resolve and a firm resolution among Amish leaders to do whatever needs to be done to follow the Biblical dictate to remain *"different"* from the *"world"* and to keep families together while preserving the "spirit of yesteryear" in every facet of their lives.

The Amish leaders, after much thought and deliberation, will permit the adoption of a new invention, a modern product or perhaps a new kitchen gadget (almost always altered in some manner) for members' use if it meets the following criteria:

1. Will it bring about increased interaction with the "English" and thus result in more exposure to secular values and lead to moral decay (i.e., TV, radio, the internet and mass media would bring about such exposure) among members?

2. Will it assist in keeping members dependent on God and one

another, humble, obedient and not result in the development of personal pride?

3. Would permitting the use of a certain new device, even if altered somewhat from the original, translate to a negative effect on Amish values, community stability or cultural identity?

4. Will it safeguard the current social status and equality among members?

5. Can the specific compromise with progress be positively viewed in light of Amish history? Is it a "fit" for their culture?

6. What will it mean for the future of the community? Will it lead to even more unwanted, advanced products being desired by community members?

7. Most importantly, will the adoption of something new, regardless of how it is altered, still allow the Amish to remain *"different"* from the *"world,"* to be a *"peculiar"* people (Titus 2:14) and to not *"conform"* to the *"world?"*

Outsiders view many of the Amish culture's compromises with progress as an odd, confusing mixture of tradition and twenty-first century modernism. Others see such compromises as down right silly, ridiculous, inconsistent, baffling, perplexing and extremely puzzling. For example, I am often asked how the Amish church can possibly justify riding in a car while not permitting members' to own one. How can the church strictly forbid telephones being installed in members' homes yet endorse the use of a community pay phone (known as the Amish phone shanty)? How can bicycles be taboo but scooters acceptable **(Note, the Amish boy on the cover of this book is riding a scooter that has been altered with larger than normal wheels)?** How can the church sanction bus and train travel (when necessary) but strictly forbid traveling by air? As I attempt to explain below, these compromises with twenty-first century progress may be confusing to non-Amish, but to the Amish they are reasonable, consistent and logical and in keeping with their creed to be *"different from the world"* in every facet of their lives.

"No" to Electricity but "Yes" to 12 Volt Batteries

How can the Amish reconcile shunning electrically but yet permitting the use of a 12 vote battery to power certain tools and products? When electricity became commonplace before the middle of the 20th Century, the Amish leaders were convinced that a linking with non-Amish via electrical wires would constitute a counter-to-the-*Bible*, seamless connection, to be *"yoked"* with the *"world"* and *"non-believers."* That decision has continuously protected the Amish from outside influences such as those that would be brought into the community via television, the internet, etc. And, as the Amish view it, a battery is not directly connected or linked (via wires or otherwise) in any manner to "worldly" people. However, transistor radios, battery powered CD players and many other such products are not acceptable.

There are some appliances that the *"world"* operates via electricity that the Amish convert to run efficiently on natural gas. To the Amish, the important word here is "natural" in that it is not man-made. However, many Old Order Amish families with whom the writer is acquainted, still use coal or wood burning heating and cooking stoves and an "icebox" instead of a gas refrigerator.

Wind and water power are acceptable to the Old Order because they are a natural, God made source of power and not connected to man made power lines. To them, generating power in this natural manner is *"different"* from the way the *"world"* generates its power and is thus not *"conforming"* to the ways of the *"world!"* Hypothetically speaking, it may be that, if and when society at large switches from electricity to atomic power or some other alternative power, the Amish may consider the use of electricity.

No Telephones in the Home But Using One is Permitted

Having a phone installed in one's home is prohibited but the Amish church permits telephone use on a limited basis. As noted above, most Amish church districts permit the use of the pay phone that has been conveniently installed within their communities. Such phones (as well as the English neighbor's phone) are to be used for "important" business or emergency reasons only and not for incoming calls (however, some of these special pay phones do contain message machines). Anyone using the telephone for casual visiting with another would find themselves in conflict with the orders of their church.

Some Amish church districts do permit members to install phones in the barn or in a farm shed for business purposes. And, in some districts, the member is given permission to answer these "barn" phones only at certain times during the working day and never on Sunday. I recently received a business call from an Amish man using his barn phone. I was unavailable to take the call and he left a message indicating that he would only answer the barn phone between the hours of 4 and 7 AM Monday through Saturday! Again, to the Amish, this is a reasonable and logical compromise with progress and coincides perfectly with the criteria given above.

A phone in a participant's home is viewed as a real threat to face-to face-visits so highly valued by the Amish (As mentioned elsewhere, church is held every other week with the in between Sunday set aside for visiting purposes). In addition, home based phones would permit unwanted "English" intrusions into the Amish home as well as providing an unfavorable link to the outside world. Amish leaders are convinced that phones in the home would disrupt their slow-paced, stress free lives and negatively effect the stability of their little communities. But, according to an Amish minister friend, the most damaging aspect would be that of Amish children having the opportunity to engage in idle chit chat with Amish, and maybe even non-Amish, friends. I am convinced that the Amish leaders will remain steadfast in their refusal to permit the installation of phones in members' homes.

Using Tractors in the Barn Yard But Not in the Fields

Non-Amish are perplexed with the notion that several Amish church districts permit their members to own a modern tractor for use around the barnyard but it can never be used in the fields. Some also permit the use of modern farm equipment that is altered and pulled in the fields by teams of horses. Some Amish church districts permit tractors but they must have the wheels removed, mounted on a wagon, and pulled from job to job by a team of horses! While driving through an Amish county side you may also see a piece of up-to-date, modern farm equipment being powered by a diesel engine mounted on top of it, being pulled across a field by a team of horses.

The use of horses to do field work automatically limits the expansion and size of farms. Amish leaders are convinced that large farms would result in personal greed, power and personal pride. But, most damaging of all, the ownership of large farms would upset the social status, member equality and thus the stability of the community. "Lead us not into temptation" is an often cited prayer among the Amish and the ministers work hard at trying to insure that members are "tempted" as little as possible. For example, the "barn yard" tractors are always outfitted with steel wheels which keeps the owner *"different"* but also from being "tempted" to drive it to town or perhaps to the neighbor's house. Amish leaders believe that permitting such leisure driving of the tractor would result in members then desiring to own pick-up trucks or perhaps even cars (Criteria #6 above)?

As discussed elsewhere in this book, many Amish are now engaged in home enterprises due to the increasing cost of farmland. Again, in an attempt to regulate the growth of these home based enterprises, Amish church districts have limited the number of outside-the-family employees allowed by each business to a minimal number, usually 3 or 4 individuals. Again, this may seem inconsistent and silly to some, but to the Amish, it is a "fit" for maintaining their way of life.

Ownership of a Car is Taboo But Riding in One is Permitted

Many modern inventions, devices, home telephones, farm equipment, etc. are forbidden because Amish church leaders are concerned about the long time consequences of adapting such modern conveniences. And as noted above, some of these "taboos" are difficult for many non-Amish to comprehend and understand. However, the manner in which the Amish view the automobile may be the most perplexing of all contradictions to non-Amish individuals.

Several Amish leaders have told me that there is nothing inherently wrong with the automobile, per se, but that the consequences of **owning** one would be extremely detrimental to the Amish way of life! They are especially concerned about the detrimental effects owning a car would have on their youth and future generations. Owning a car would result in members having easy access to the "English" and to possible association with "non believers." Such close association would, the ministers believe, result in members being led "astray" spiritually and perhaps even away from the church. The Amish leaders are convinced that such ownership would lead to members' developing more "worldly" needs and wants that could then not be met within the confines of the Amish community. Amish leaders are also convinced that owning a car would negatively effect the slow-paced, patient, stress free lifestyle valued so highly by the community. They also realize that the owning of a car would make it too easy for members to have access to faraway places and would challenge the concept of a small community of believers visiting and worshiping together. Owning an automobile, the leaders fear, would introduce speed, mobility and social status problems now conspicuously absent within their society. But most importantly, it would lead to members' developing self pride and gaining autonomy and independence, among the most dreaded of taboo characteristics.

The owner of an automobile would also be required to obtain a drivers license which would necessitate having a forbidden photo taken. In addition, having a drivers license similiar to a "worldly" person, would automatically cause one to be *"unequally yoked"* with the non-believers.

A forever present and highly valued symbol of Amish cultural identity is the fact that they travel by horse and buggy. Not owning automobiles insures that the group will maintain this most important of all Amish symbols—the horse. In sum, not permitting the ownership of a car is a significant boundary maintaining device that distinctively separates the Amish from the "English" society that surrounds them. And, in America, not owning a car most certainly keeps them *"different"* from the rest of us!

It is becoming more and more common to see Old Order Amish individuals riding in a car being driven by a non-Amish person. In such cases, a hired "English" driver most likely owns the car (they are not permitted to ride in a former church member's car). If a specific situation or event requires automobile transportation, such travel is then sanctioned and permissible. Sometimes a trip must be taken to a distant Amish community for a funeral or wedding and the Bishops will have given their approval to use a hired driver for such occasions. In addition, the Amish will pay for rides to meet various transportation needs such as travel to outside employment or for medical attention if the distance is prohibitive or too dangerous for horse and buggy travel. Although it may be viewed as inconsistent to non-Amish individuals, the "car compromise" makes perfect sense to the Amish. It maintains their way of life while yet permitting members a small, modern convenience and enhances the "horse and buggy" concept of cultural identity.

As noted, following much thought and extensive deliberation, an Amish church district may agree to permit members the use of a controversial modern kitchen device, new invention or whatever. However, the same church leaders may suddenly change their minds about the use of this same device. That is, if the church leaders suddenly agree that the continued use of a specific "progressive" device is a detriment to their society, they will, without fanfare, immediately outlaw its further use.

I understand why the above described compromises are puzzling to the average non-Amish person. To many, the Amish are walking a delicate, thin, almost hypocritical line in their zeal to remain *"separate from the world."* However, an empathic viewing of these compromises with progress through the eyes of the Amish, reveals that they are simply remaining steadfast to the Biblical dictate to be *"different"* from the *"world"* while not jeopardizing their "old" way of life. And, the Amish endorse all such compromises with the confidence that they are still following the most important of their Biblical dictates: *"...be in but not of the world."* Many more such compromises with the modern world that seem puzzling to the non-Amish could be given here.

Epilogue

I have chosen to focus on the positive aspects of the Amish and their way of life in this book. Is there a negative side to the Amish and to their way of life? Does this culture have any negative attributes? The answer is, of course, "yes" to both questions.

The Amish are not immune from many of the problems and concerns that other non-Amish Americans face on a day to day basis. And, most certainly, the problems facing their youth, for example, are similar to those facing all youth in the fast paced world of the 21st Century. As mentioned elsewhere in this book, many Amish youth go through a "running around time," (known as *rum springa* among the Amish) just prior to baptism and some run into difficulty with the *"world"* during this phase of their life. That is, they tend to experiment with, as the Amish say, some of the "frivolous" aspects of the modern world. Interestingly, it is from among this group of Amish youth that newspaper, magazine, and TV reporters almost always obtain their sources for material regarding the Amish. Thus, what is written about the Amish is often inaccurate and skewed since those being interviewed are youth that are in a temporary, but somewhat rebellious stage of their life. Baptized members of the church would be a better, more reliable source for the reporters, but, of course, they are prohibited from conducting such interviews. I wish to acknowledge that most Amish teenagers (some 80% or more) negotiate *rum springa* safely and grow into Amish adulthood eager to submit to the strictures of the Amish church.

Now that you have read my book it also quite obvious that I, although no longer Amish, am a staunch defender of the Amish and their chosen way of life. That is, I believe strongly that they have a constitutional right to live their lives in the new century in the *"peculiar and different"* way they choose. And, I believe that they should be permitted to do so without any interference from the non-Amish American public and/or from our government. As I stated in Section I, the Amish immigrated to the United States at the invitation of William Penn to take part in his "religious experiment" and have managed, not only to survive, but also to prosper. However, God fearing, *"defenseless Christian"* groups such as the Amish, who continue to *"turn the other cheek"* as dictated by their religious faith, will lose most every religious battle in which they engage the secular society unless someone "defends" them. That is, since they will not defend themselves, their survival will continue to depend on assistance from non-Amish defenders. As written elsewhere, I have defended, and will continue to defend, this small religious sects' right to religious freedom in America. And, so long as they continue to make the excellent contributions they now make to the greater, mainstream secular society, pay their taxes, are not harmful to others, etc., I will vigorously continue to do so.

I have defended the *"defenseless Christian"* Amish in several court cases during which time I served as their spokesperson. As noted, a group such as the Amish needs a non-Amish spokesperson since they will not, as dictated in the *Bible*, defend themselves in any manner. However, the personal contribution I value most is the assistance I gave them regarding the U.S. Supreme Court decision which exempted their children from having to attend our public high schools. This was an historic decision and, although various small religious groups had/have made similar attempts, no other group has, to this date, gained this right for their children.

I was elated with the Supreme Court's decision at the time and am very proud of the small role I played in this historic accomplishment. Seeking to have their children exempted from having to attend and face the daily contaminating influences of the American high school was not a "fly by night" maneuver on the part of the Amish. That is, the pious, horse and buggy Amish have disapproved of their offspring attending public high school for more than a hundred years. I am happy that it is not only legitimate to be Old Order Amish in America today, but also that the Supreme

Court's decision, along with several other legal decisions since, makes it constitutionally legitimate to be reared as one!

It is difficult to measure the total affect that America's progress has on a people such as the Amish who are committed to a primitive technology in the midst of a modern world bent on secularization and an even more fast-paced approach to every day life. However, the Amish are a tenacious people and are intent on maintaining their way of life. Family and closeness to one another is everything to the peaceful Amish. With those ties they have survived in America for over 300 years. Now, in the new millennium, the land offered to them by William Penn is cluttered, costly and offers little accommodation for their way of life. However, as described elsewhere, they are adapting as needed so as to maintain and enhance their way of life.

Is the Amish struggle for religious freedom in America now a thing of the past? No, as noted in several places in this book, there are several ongoing battles that, unless the Amish prevail, will undermine their way of life and make it difficult for them to remain in America. I anticipate that many more such struggles between the Amish and the modern *"world"* will be forthcoming. It is extremely difficult for them to "stay the same" in Twenty-first Century America. As our secular society becomes even faster paced and computer driven, it will be even more difficult for the Old Order Amish to maintain their slow paced, closed society within our fast-paced secular society. That is, unless we are willing to find ways to accommodate them and their way of life. And, I hope this book will convince others that they are worth saving for America! They offer a way of life, a simple way of living that may just one day, in the not too distant future, be viewed as a very important, viable alternative by the *"world."*

However, I believe strongly that the Amish will do whatever is necessary to preserve their faith and sustain the family. I also predict that the Old Order Amish will continue to grow in number in America. I sincerely believe that my Amish heritage will continue to be a source of satisfaction and enjoyment to your descendents and mine for years to come. That is, they will not only survive as a closed society within our ever changing, fast-paced secular society, they will prosper in the new millennium and gain new respect from the *"world"* for doing so.